心田的耕耘者

— 許其正的創作歲月

魯　蛟等著

文　學　叢　刊

文史哲出版社印行

國家圖書館出版品預行編目資料

心田的耕耘者：許其正的創作歲月 / 魯蛟等
著 .-- 初版 --臺北市：文史哲，民 108.06
　頁；　公分 .-- （文學叢刊；406）
ISBN 978-986-314-469-4 （平裝）

1.許其正　2.新詩　3.詩評

863.21　　　　　　　　　　　　　108008745

文　學　叢　刊　406

心 田 的 耕 耘 者
── 許其正的創作歲月

著　　　者：魯　　　　　　　蛟　等
出　版　者：文　史　哲　出　版　社
http：//www.lapen.com.tw
e-mail：lapen@ms74.hinet.net
登記證字號：行政院新聞局版臺業字五三三七號
發　行　人：彭　　　正　　　雄
發　行　所：文　史　哲　出　版　社
印　刷　者：文　史　哲　出　版　社
臺北市羅斯福路一段七十二巷四號
郵政劃撥帳號：一六一八○一七五
電話886-2-23511028・傳真886-2-23965656

定價新臺幣三五○元

二○一九年（民一○八）六 月 初 版
二○一九年（民一○八）八月初版二刷

著財權所有・侵權者必究
ISBN 978-986-314-469-4　　　10406

小言幾句

許其正

　　適逢《華文現代詩》五周年既「三界公」八十誕辰，陳福成執筆，給華文所有成員各寫了一本評介，我也忝列其一。這讓我想起，一些作家、評論家這些年來給我的評論文章，乃集結起來，趁此時予以出版。出版前，我想說幾句話。

　　我的第一本著作詩集《半天鳥》於一九六四年出版。當時引出一些評論。最早寫評的是寒爵和當時我不知為何方神聖幾年後才發現是林鐘隆的林舒。其後，幾乎每出版一本書都引來評論。這本書就是收集那些評論的總集精選。因為集成後，發現文章太多，印起來篇幅太大，乃予刪削。刪削後的這些文章，大約是總數的一半多些。

　　謹借用無名卒和魯蛟的評文綜合成為書名。書中作者分布世界各國，篇章是依文章發表的時間先後為序。文章內文，中英文甚至希臘文、馬爾他文都有，有些是中外文對照，主要是為盡量保留原發表的樣貌，文後都標有發表的刊物名和日期。至於獲推薦諾貝爾文學獎候選人那篇的文本則因陳福成寫的那本評介已收入，予以從缺。

當時寫評文的作者，有的是本來就熟識的，有的則是素昧平生，如利物浦的約翰・弗朗西斯・米塞特（John Francis Missett）、印度的辛格（R.K.Singh）和藍姆・薩爾馬（Dr. Ram Sharma）、重慶的唐詩、以色列的露紮・卡羅爾（Luiza Carol）、馬爾他的派翠克・薩瑪（Patrick J. Sammut）等；時光不待人，到現在則有的已失去連繫，如溫筆良、羊牧、林野、約翰・弗朗西斯・米塞特等，有的已登天界，如寒爵、林舒、無名卒、王式儉等；我當時是廿幾歲的小夥子，現在則已年屆八十的老人。趁這因緣，把這些評文出版印行，或可保留些蛛絲馬跡吧！如能把失去連繫的找回來，則更是一天大的收穫，將使我高興不置。

我要在這裡特別感謝評文的作者，也請愛護我的親友多多指教。

心田的耕耘者
—— 許其正的創作歲月

魯　蛟　等著

目　次

新詩的趨向

——由「半天鳥」談起

寒　爵

　　我在少年時代，曾偷偷地寫過詩。我之所以「偷偷」，是因為沒有人教導，沒有人指點，自己把過剩的情感，偷偷地記在紙上，用自己的喜悅，來彩飾自己的靈魂，總覺得那長短行裡跳躍著青春的氣息。

　　年齡漸漸大了，情感褪色了，寫詩的興趣也淡了；但我還是喜歡詩，遇到好的詩，總覺得內心裡有一種快感。不過近年來，因為「魘魔派」的詩，用「鬼畫符」的方式，迷亂著讀者的心，我為了怕著魔，索性連詩都懶得看了！

　　不久前，本省籍青年詩人許其正君寄給我一本「半天鳥」，又引起了我讀詩的興趣。讀過一遍之後，彷彿我又回到少年時代，重拾起遺失了很久的「喜悅」。

　　「半天鳥」裡所收的詩，並沒有「魘魔派」詩人所自誇的「越使人看不懂越好」的辭句。它樸實，純真，平易之中涵有深奧的哲理；沒有世紀末的頹廢病度；充滿了生命的活力。我一向不願對人做溢美之詞，相信我這些話是憑我做為一個讀者的良知而說的。

　　在全詩集中，像「果樹園的呼喚」、「土城子的夢」、「音樂的姿影」「在諧音中」、「陽光花園」、「我們向前走著」、「半天鳥」……都是好詩；我尤其喜歡「山」，一股雄渾之氣，籠罩全詩。像：

> 「頂著藍天，頂著白雲，頂著星
> 時時沉思
> 沉思善，沉思生命
> 化熱情為靈，隨風而去
> 去向遠方
> 播予虛無，播予理想
> 啊，山，沉默的山
> 啊，山，永恆的山
> 默坐無言，如禪中的佛
> 啊，山就是山」

　　句子是經過千錘百鍊的，雄渾中帶有美感。
　　在「半天鳥」詩集中的特點，就是除了巧妙地運用平常語句之外，又能靈活地運用故有的言語。例如：「像吃了人仙果，我全身舒暢」，是引用自「老殘遊記」；如「鸙鶹在外，不得而入。」是引用自「鏡花緣」；又如「草木生焉，鳥獸棲焉」等，又是把經書裡的詞句加以變化運用的。只要運用得恰當，一切言語都可以入詩。當然，這又非「笑了，齒齒齒，哭了，窗窗窗」濫唱魔調者所能想像了！

詩是有靈性，且必須有靈性的。沒有靈性的詩，只是骷髏的跳舞，字句的堆砌而已！讀後枯燥無聊，正是所謂「味同嚼蠟」。不過，現在的新詩人們，往往喜歡玩弄文字的把戲，絞盡了腦汁，想法使人看不懂；看不懂的就是好詩。他們說：「詩是寫給我自己看的，你看不懂，是你不懂得詩；我也並不需要你看得懂。」既然是寫給自己看的，為什麼發表呢？他們並沒有交代。

我總覺得，真正的好詩，不在於使人看不懂，而在於有無靈性，有無意境。所謂「詩中有畫」的詩，在古典詩中並不是生辭僻字的堆砌；一個詩人若刻意於「使人看不懂」，他的詩和他的「詩的生命」，無論他如何自詡自誇，也如水寫的名字，一瞬即逝的。

英國浪漫派詩人華茲華斯的詩，有田園的素樸的氣質；他擷取平凡的日常生活中的故事和情景，用平易的日常語言，創造出平實而有力的詩篇。他說：「這些田園生活的人們所用的語言，盡可能地應用進去。」並未因用平凡的語言入詩，而減低了他詩的價值，降低了他享譽百年的詩名。

　　詩人有敏銳的感觸，對於人生，對於自然，有比常人更深一層的認識。習於真，近於善，止於美。所謂「從一粒沙中看大千世界。」正是詩人精神領域的活動寫照。

　　新詩的形式縱然學自西洋詩，但是必須創造出一種涵有民族性格的中國詩來；從形式到內容一味盲目追求「西化」的，無疑是一種由自卑而自棄的墮落。

　　　　　　　　1964 年 8 月 22~23 日徵信新聞報「人間」
　　　　　　　　1964 年 10 月臺灣文藝

　　按:本文作者本名韓道誠，作家，曾任國立編館編審，已故。

一本可讀的詩集

——評「半天鳥」

林　舒

　　很多年沒有耐心讀完一本詩集了，往往讀了一半或一半多些就丟棄。或有些詩讀到完，有些詩讀了一些就放過去。因為難懂、不懂，所以生厭了。可是很難得的，最近，我讀完了一本詩集——「半天鳥」，這也不是為什麼，只因為這一本是可讀的詩集，讀得懂的詩集。

　　年輕時候很喜歡詩，也讀了不少詩，也寫過詩，只是因為那時候，國文程度差，寫詩寫不好。後來的詩，據詩人們自己的說法，是「現代」化了，於是漸漸地難懂了，讀都讀不懂了，也就不敢寫了。有很多本是喜歡詩的人，就這樣與詩漸漸地疏遠了，看到詩，篇篇要讀的，偶而才讀了，偶而才讀的，根本不讀了。這是詩人的悲哀，詩的悲哀。我覺得這是因為詩人們漸漸地走進了象牙之塔的結果。也許詩人們不承認這一點，要說是

讀者的程度跟不上詩的進步。而這一本詩集，也許由於
作者還年輕的緣故，還沒有把自己關進象牙之塔裡去。

　　據我所知，這是許其正的處女詩集。除附錄不算
外，共收入二十八首詩。二十八首雖不多，要藉此窺見
詩人的容貌，是十分地足夠了。因為一個詩人就是坦率
地把他自己描繪出來了。古人說：詩言志。其實言志的
又何止是詩？一切文學作品，都蘊含著，透察著作者的
心靈，因此，作者的心靈的高尚與鄙賤，美好與醜惡，
決定了他的詩質，這詩質鄙賤、醜惡的，決不會是好詩。
讓我抄幾句，來看看作者的詩質吧：

　　　　進來讓鳥語從菓樹的枝葉間滴下
　　　　然後輕輕地敲響你的耳鼓
　　　　讓那些不快和憂傷離你遠去
　　　　讓美音的世界把喜悅奉獻給你
　　　　　　──菓樹園的呼喚

　　　　春風遍吻大地，輕撫大地
　　　　無數美花齊放，五彩繽紛
　　　　無數歡笑齊放，叮叮噹噹

　　　　啊，叮叮噹噹

無數歡笑在唱
唱出朵朵春天，朵朵美和愛

從這些，我們窺見了什麼？讓我們看看作者在「後記」的自剖的話：

「與其說『半天鳥』這集子寫我的童年，倒不如說表現我童年那些天真無邪、無憂無愁及和平快樂、美麗安靜而充滿陽光和歡笑的境界。」

這種作者所追求的理想，這些作者心靈的美好的意念，我們在全集中，幾乎任何一首詩裡都可以感覺到可愛清純無垢的美。懷抱著這種心靈的作者，只要忠實於他的心靈，所寫出來的詩，一定會很令人喜悅的。

看來作者似乎一味地在追求理想，注意的是遠景，其實也不盡然，作者仍舊立腳於現實中，有不少是很實際的，如：

呼一聲健康的「嘟」，
我便運動體力，拔腿出發
——沿著一定的軌道。
　　——火車頭

你看後一句，是多麼實際而有力的暗示！
又如：

明天我還有許多許多事情
所以現在我必須不斷地工作
　　　　──兩行一束

蔗尾飼牛去！
蔗葉蓋厝、燒火、做肥料去！
蔗幹榨糖去！
渣滓燒火、製蔗板、做肥料去！
　　　　──任你撕去身心吸去血，
我只是一心想貢獻給人類！
　　　　　　──甘蔗的話

沒有任何怨言　也沒有淚
每天不停地工作　為要完成本分
　　　　──織布機

這些都是非常實際的作者的望想，是溫和的，多麼
溫和的勸慰或呼喚！

我還喜歡這樣的描寫：

進來靠著樹幹坐在菓樹下
和碧茵分啖樹蔭的層層清涼
　　　──菓樹園的呼喚

柔光瀰漫著，像籠罩著透明玻璃的細絲絨織就的
網，每一個網孔都盛開著花朵，燦爛，典麗，光彩輝煌……
　　　──月的世界

我覺得這些描寫很美。
作者在用詞，造句上，也有他的特色，如：

利欲利欲不了山
冷暖冷暖不了山
　　　──山

這兩個轉為動詞的詞，用得很俐落，一點不會牽強。
又如：

媽媽有媽媽要唸的媽媽經
媽媽有媽媽要做的媽媽事

　　媽媽有媽媽特有的媽媽心腸
　　媽媽有媽媽特有的媽媽個性

　　媽媽常把媽媽的善良教給媽媽的孩子
　　媽媽常把媽媽的溫和傳給媽媽的孩子
　　　　──媽媽曲

　像這種口語化的句子，讀來頗為新穎可愛。
「詩境」裡的這樣的句子也是我很欣賞的：

　　陽光普照，閃閃發光
　　閃閃發光啊光芒萬丈
　　光芒萬丈啊燦爛輝煌

　這幾個句子，不但讀來音韻和諧美妙，而且音調步
步加強，表現出陽光的熱與力的步步增高。
　「晨」這首詩的音調也是很美的：

　　繫著一個鈴鐺
　　一步一聲響
　　晨，從朝露中來了

來了，自東方

自東方；叮噹
響一聲，閃一次光亮
叮噹，自東方
響一聲，發一次熱量

閃一次光亮
群樹便一次昂頭凝望
發一次熱量
生命便一次跳動震盪

叮噹，晨來了
叮噹，白日的輪子轉了
鈴鐺同時伴著響
叮噹，叮噹，叮噹……

「山」的第一節，我也很喜愛：

山，沉默的山
蘊足以融化南極最大冰海的熱情
而顯堅毅與冷靜於外

化熱情為靈，隨風而去
去向遠方
播予虛無，播予理想
山無言
默坐，如禪中的佛
啊，山就是山

　　我喜歡的是作者不是直接去描繪山，而是寫出透過心靈所見的山，因而似在寫山，卻寫出了一個人生相，也是作者心中理想的人生的一種相貌。

　　「山」的末節，大致與第一節一樣，只是，作者在第三行與第四行中間加了：

頂著藍天，頂著白雲，頂著星
時時沉思
沉思善，沉思生命

　　而把第七行的「山無言」換成：

啊，山，沉默的山
山，永恆的山

　　從加入的句子，我們更可窺見作者如何用勁地鼓吹他的可愛的人生理想了。

　　最後，我覺得作者用「半天鳥」做為本集的名字，可以說最恰當不過了。因為作者自身，就是名副其實的半天鳥，他立足於現實，卻嚮往於理想，而努力在現實及理想之間搭一座無形的，心靈的橋樑。

　　他說：

　　　我是一隻嬌小的半天鳥，
　　　展開翅，冉冉地往上升，
　　　在夏午，迎著靜熱的藍空。

　　他就這樣子離開現實，開始飛揚。為理想歌唱：

　　　翢的一聲：飛，我也開始唱，
　　　唱出南方之歌，唱得空氣聲聲震盪。
　　　——半天裡起一陣風浪。

　　但是，作者又說：

　　　飛得疲了，唱得啞了，
　　　風浪便將我旋翢地上，

醺醺地睡去，不顧一切。

他就是這樣天真無邪。但是

待我甦醒，從遠地的夢中，
天仍舊藍、靜，地還是悶、熱；
只不見那一陣半天裡的風浪。

清醒的時候，他不曾一刻忘懷他要做的事。於是他又奔赴他心目中理想的聖壇。他唱著：

我是一隻嬌小的半天鳥，
展開翅，冉冉地往上昇，
在夏午，迎著靜熱的藍空。

這隻半天鳥，正是一個青年人的化身，不是嗎？

我覺得這是一本「可愛的」詩集。好的詩，一方面要能深入，一方面又要能淺出，淺出，才能雅俗共賞，才能擁有廣大的讀者；深入才能搖撼人的心靈，越嚼越甘而其味無窮。淺出，是讀得懂，可讀的要素，作者在這一點，似乎很注意，但有些地方，表現得太直率了，似乎還須要含蓄些。至於深入這一點，我相信，作者定能好好致力，會與其年齡經驗與日俱增，與日俱進的。

　　散文也好，小說也好，詩也好；現代也罷，古典也罷；浪漫主義也好，我以為什麼都沒有關係，可讀，能懂，這才是要緊的。詩，要努力使成為文藝愛好者所普遍愛好的東西，若成為詩人們自己的讀物，甚至於甲詩人讀不懂乙詩人的詩，不是悲哀，也叫人可憐的。因此，讀了「半天鳥」，使我覺得，我這個曾愛好過詩的人，並未被所有的詩人擯斥於詩園之外，感到莫大的喜慰。

1964 年 10 月臺灣文藝

　　按：本文作者本名林鍾隆，作家，擅寫散文、新詩、兒童文學，曾任教師，已故。

理性和感性集一身　許其正寫盡田園風味

溫筆良

　　許其正的人正如他的散文和詩一樣，文質彬彬的，充滿鄉野田園味道。他不算是一位多產作家，但是欣賞他的作品，猶如郊遊踏青，令人清新愉快。

　　許其正，四十三歲，潮州鎮人，畢業於東吳大學法律系，現任潮州光春國中教務主任。大學一年級就開始寫文章，到現在為止已經出版了六本散文與詩的單行本。新詩集「半天鳥」和「菩薩心」。散文集「樹苗」、「綠園散記」、「綠蔭深處」及「夏蔭」。

　　法律是理性而冷靜的，散文詩詞卻是感性而豪放的，這二者是如何集於他的一身呢？他推推方形褐色的鏡框，露出整齊的牙齒笑著說：「這大概是聯考填志願所造成的吧！我的確非常酷愛文學，大二時曾想轉到中文系去，但是終究沒那麼做。學法律帶給我的是，現在拿著公民課本給學生上做人處世的道理。但，我還是偏向文藝的。教學生讀古文，寫文章，找尋我的樂趣。」

　　在東吳一年級起，就開始寫文章，曾經嘗試著寫小說，但，終歸難以壓抑對散文與詩的偏愛，因此，這類作品發表的較多，成集列冊出了六本單行本。

　　「寫詩與散文需要靈感與蘊釀的環境，但是下筆寫作時，卻不會讓外界吵雜的環境干擾到作品的形成。『綠蔭深處』就是在當時很轟動的一部連續劇『保鑣』上演時完成的。家人在看電視，我就在一邊運思爬格子，高潮迭起的劇情，不會影響到我寫作的情緒與進度。」

　　許其正從小在充滿泥土味的鄉間長大，因此，作品的內容也多半都是描寫大自然鄉野田園的人事物。正如他在「夏蔭」序文中說的「我總愛搬張籐椅在夏蔭裡坐著，避開那些烈陽，揮去那些燠熱，摒除那些煩躁、沉悶、疲倦和不快；讓清涼、舒適、和諧和寧靜陪伴著我，讓那些喜悅和平和圍繞著我……。」

　　多年來沉浸在文藝世界裡，也塑造了他喜好沉思、寧靜的個性，談吐舉止洋溢著濃鬱的書卷氣。他喜歡寫詩，更愛讀詩，尤其是別人意境優美富有內涵的詩，他主張一首好詩應該是主題表達正確，真正發揮了詩簡短而意境深遠的境界，像西班牙西摩尼的作品「小毛驢與我」，他一讀再讀，品嚐清新、活潑、富有田園意味的內涵。國內作家張秀亞、蕭白的作品他也常拜讀。

　　有些新詩跳躍出一般人的想像領會之外，令人難以理解。有的斷句斷章式的分別各自獨立，整篇意旨難以貫穿；或者詞句非常華麗，但內容卻貧瘠空洞，他認為這都不是好的作品，也非寫詩的正途。

　　閒暇，他喜歡郊遊，看些散文和其他的書籍，以及打排球及桌球。

1982 年 12 月 12 日屏東週刊

　　按：本文作者為新聞工作者，曾創辦《屏東週刊》，擔任主
　　編。

欣賞「夏蔭」

林清泉

　　「我總愛搬張籐椅在夏蔭裡坐著，避開那些烈陽，揮去那些燠熱，摒除那些煩躁、沉悶、疲倦和不快；讓清涼、舒適、和諧和寧靜陪伴著我，讓那些喜悅和平和圍繞著我。」這是從「夏蔭」裡摘錄的一段話，道出了作者的人生哲學以及他追求的寫意生涯。

　　「夏蔭」是詩人許其正先生的散文自選集，共選輯了八十多篇作品，分成三輯，一輯是穭苗，二輯是綠園散記，三輯是綠蔭深處。在台灣，以詩人兼寫散文的不少，許其正便是其中的一位。他寫作很勤，詩與散文發表得很多，他的散文具有他特殊的風格，簡潔、清新，有詩意，帶有濃濃的鄉土情懷。篇幅很短，就以本書的作品來說，長的很少超過千字，短的祇有數百字，有幾篇乍讀起來簡直是詩。

　　作者出身農村，所寫的是他熟稔的農村景色、原野的風光，兒時的回憶；他用真摯的情感，靈活的筆觸把這些題材描述得生動活現，歷歷在目，成了動態美麗的畫面，讀後令人心馳神往。

如他寫農村的豐收：「整個村子的人歡笑著，他們為豐收而歡笑。整個村子的人忙碌著，他們為豐收而忙碌。看見他們，我的心裡掀起了一片歡呼：啊，豐收！豐收！」「田地裡，稻浪翻風，在太陽下閃爍金黃亮光。割稻的人猛揮鐮刀。脫穀機聲猛響。麻袋一袋袋地裝滿，穀子一車車地運回家。看見這些，我的心裡掀起了一片歡呼：啊，豐收！豐收！」把農村收割時，由於是豐收，使農人忘了勞累，充滿了一片快樂的景象，呈現在讀者的面前。

如他寫早晨的林間：「早晨，林間是一座鳥的音樂園。當晨曦才從東方大武山頂款步而來，群鳥便開始展放歌喉了。白頭翁不用說了，斑鳩、青苔仔、麻雀、烏嘴鶲仔、黑頸藍鶲、黃鶯等等，都盡情地歡唱著，如開音樂會，輪番演奏，齊聲鳴唱，令人耳不暇聞；時而是一支雄壯的進行曲，時而是一支抒情小調，時而是一曲交響樂，時而是急管繁弦，時而是『大珠小珠落玉盤』，時而是滔滔巨浪，時而是潺潺小溪流水，時而是獨奏，時而是輪唱，時而是獨自高歌，時而是合唱……其實，那怎麼是人間的音樂？它是大自然的美音，大自然的珍品，用人間的音樂來形容，無論如何貼切，都是一種褻瀆！」把鳥在林間活動的情態，刻劃得維妙維肖，讀之眼前盡是鳥的畫面，耳際盡是鳥的鳴唱聲音。

　　讀這本書猶如在「夏蔭」裡乘涼，那些美麗的章篇，珠璣的句子，就像陣陣的涼風拂在臉上，心裡覺得清涼、舒適、喜悅、寧靜。你是否也想享受這境界呢？

　　　　　　1983 年 3 月 8 日台灣新聞報「西子灣」

　　按：本文作者曾任教師，作家，擅寫散文，兼及詩與兒童文學，已退休，後轉攻書法。

草地郎的農村組曲

羊　牧

　　去年的十二月廿五日，為期兩天的中、南部青年文藝作家座談會在高雄的佛光山舉行。那是我和許其正兄第一次見面，雖然早在我的初中時代，已常常拜讀他在各報副刊上發表的清新可喜的小品。

　　回來以後，蒙他不棄，寄贈詩集「菩提心」和散文集「夏蔭」各乙冊。這幾天學校放寒假，我有更多的時間做自己喜歡做的事，乃把兩本書拿出來仔細拜讀。

　　走在寫作的路途上，許其正兄起步得早，成就很可觀；後學如我，不敢侈言「評論」他的作品。倒是在目前文藝思潮普遍流於紊亂多歧的今日，他的散文和詩所散發的清新樸實、明快健康的風格，實有激濁揚清的作用。所以不揣簡陋，握筆抒寫一己的讀後心得。

　　許其正寫詩，是把它當做一種「永恆的事業」，他主張擴大寫作的領域，不但自己要做多項實驗，同時也要能「容忍實驗的作品」。至於「現代」這個名詞，他的界定是：

「現代必須在任何時刻都是，不要只現代一兩秒鐘而已。瞬息即消亡的現代，不是真正的現代。」

抱著這種觀點、理念來寫詩，許其正的詩的生命是長遠的。他的詩作品也是獨樹一格，不隨俗浮沉的。這本「菩提心」分為四輯：一、這朵蓮。二、菩提心。三、望星橋。四、白茶花。除了第四輯「白茶花」帶有濃濃的詩意的散文（姑名之為「散文詩」吧！），其他的三輯都是詩──一種真實情感的自然流露的文字。

許其正有著多感的心靈，這決定他的詩意象的豐饒，例子在他的詩作中俯拾即是，我不想多抄襲。至於他的表達技巧，除了偶爾使用排比、轉品等修辭手段之外，絕大多數都是以平易近人的文字直抒胸臆，帶給人一個寧靜和諧的境界。我們試讀他的「住在妳心上」一詩：

「我住在一個可愛的地方。
那裡沒有一片土，
我卻感到極為溫馨、幸福。
『嚇！到底你住在什麼地方？』
『是的，蜜子，我住在妳心上。』」

　　從三、四兩輯的詩作中，我們知道「蜜子」是詩人心田中的另一半，一旦到了「弱水三千，但取一瓢飲」的時候，詩人的情愛有了歸宿，他已進住到「蜜子」的心中，所以「沒有一片土」的地方，他卻可以「感到極為溫馨、幸福」！

　　許其正的詩就是這麼「白」，沒有艱深的字眼，也沒有誨澀難懂的技巧，讀了卻使人回味不已！

　　再說他的散文集「夏蔭」，這是他從「碎苗」、「綠園散記」、「綠蔭深處」三本散文集選輯而來的，最可以表現他散文作品的特色。

　　因為是一個詩人，所以他的散文作品中隨時流露著濃濃的詩的質素。他對意象的經營，特別喜歡用排比、頂真這些修辭的方法，一方面抒寫他纏綿不盡的情意，一方面也加深讀者的印象。

　　許其正是個土生土長的「草地郎」，他的世界裡沒有五顏六色的霓虹燈，也沒有爾虞我詐的都市人嘴臉。他寫農村在四季中的變貌，他寫鄉下人特有的多采多姿的童年，他寫鄉下人濃鬱的人情味，都提供讀者一份與世無爭、恬淡安適的心靈享受。這也正是他自選集命名為「夏蔭」的理由，因為在烈陽炙人，天氣燠熱的夏天，在夏蔭裡卻：

「沒有烈陽了，也不燠熱了，是清涼的，是舒適的，是和諧的，是寧靜的，叫人覺著喜悅而平和……」

1983 年 7 月 28 日台灣新聞報「西子灣」

按：本文作者為教師，本名廖枝春，作家，擅寫散文，後轉
　　攻台語詩及台語歌謠。

心田的耕耘者許其正

無名卒

老家那四畝地兒任其荒蕪，
卻要作心田的默默耕耘者。

有人說他像草地郎，不無幾分道理——樸拙、誠懇、低聲細語，步步踏實，誰也沒見過他穿過奇裝異服，誰也沒見過他留披頭散髮。如果不是廿年的教師生涯給他的約制，很可能天天打赤腳奔忙於田野，連買鞋子的錢也給省了。當然，這並不意味如何吝嗇，而是代表著一種樸實無華，農家子弟的天性。

有人說他又不像作家，作家往往是熱情奔放，鋒芒畢露的，甚至某些詩人，總是多少帶點狂妄與怪誕，離經叛道，脫離現實生活圈的，也大有人在。他雖然寫詩多年，卻永遠像靜海的巨輪，四平八穩地向前航行。除了輪機的節奏，從不拉一聲汽笛。

　　究竟他像什麼呢？什麼都不像，像他自己：許其正。因為能在作品中，從來不模仿別人，他也不希望別人模仿他，別人永遠是別人，他永遠是他！

　　植根於泥土，生長於泥土，田園撫育了他，他也恆久地擁抱著田園，一個學法律的人而不執著於六法全書，而緊捧著文學之鑰不放，足可說明他是怎樣的人了。真的，法律是冰涼的，文學是溫馨的，據說他讀大學時，幾度想棄法而修文，雖未如願，他並不氣餒，後來在文藝社團卻成了不可或缺的負責人，他寫詩、選稿，曾經主編過大學詩刊、雙溪、中華學刊、達德學刊、台灣文藝等等，也當過記者，服役時雖曾任軍法官職務，退役後，依然棄法從文，當起執教鞭的老師，迄今已達廿年。

　　寫作的年資比他執教的年資更久，早期作品，以新詩為主，近些年將寫作領域擴大到散文，不過我們在許其正先生的散文作品裡，很明顯地可以看到串串詩的語言，不過，許其正絕不像主張全盤「西化」的詩人，把句子抽象得只有作者自己能懂的地步。所以有人說他的詩嫌「白」，其實，人人可讀，人人願讀，人人能懂的詩，又有什麼不好？作品面世，訴諸的對象是群眾是讀者，一首大家看不懂的詩，還發表幹嗎？無名卒不是詩人，僅僅是個不上道的讀者，雖無法深入地層下去一探

「詩」的奧秘，但詩的好壞，還有幾分辨識能力，我要說：好詩不一定深奧，壞詩不一定淺顯，深奧並不代表佳構，高意境的詩作，才能代表永恆。

我們現在看看方塊名家寒爵先生，對許其正的詩集「半天鳥」所作的評語：「半天鳥」裡所寫的詩，並沒有「魘魔派」詩人所自誇的「越使人看不懂越好」的詞句，它樸實、純真、平易中涵有哲理；沒有世紀末的頹廢病度；它充滿了生命的活力，我一向不願對人做溢美之詞，相信我這些話，是憑我做為一個讀者的良心說的……。我尤其喜歡「山」，它有一股雄渾之氣：

> 頂著藍天，頂著白雲，頂著星
> 時時沉思
> 沉思善，沉思生命
> 化熱情為靈，隨風而去
> 去向遠方
> 播予虛無，播予理想
> 啊，山，沉默的山
> 山，永恆的山
> 默坐無言，如禪中的佛
> 啊，山就是山」

　　寒爵先生說他的句子是經過千錘百鍊的，雄渾中帶有美感。寒爵先生更嚴厲地借題評一些他所謂的「魑魔派」詩人的作品：「沒有靈性，是骷髏翩舞」，兩相輝映，更能讓我們體會到許詩的珍貴與難得。

　　許其正先生近期散文寫作很勤，尤其卸去主任之職以後，幾家大報上差不多每天讓讀者見面的「珠串」文章，真是精巧玲瓏的作品。有人說珠串是散文，有人說是小品，不管怎麼說，在珠串的作品裡，我們依然可以發現詩的影子。別看那每篇只有六百字的作品，日積月累，質量都很可觀！據我所知，他已集結的有半天鳥、菩提心、穭苗、綠園散記、綠蔭深處、夏蔭……等。現在手邊堆積的待印文章，仍可出好幾本書，看到他能寫出這麼多作品，誰都會認為他是精力充沛的人，其實，完全錯了！他是低血壓的患者，平常他的血壓總是徘徊在六十到九十之間。所以他長年跟疲倦戰鬥——在心理上他是勝家，在現實中他落敗了。不過，他有種睜著眼睛打瞌睡的本領，當學生時，老師不曾發現，授課時學生也不知道，在軍中的集會上，能站著打盹不被發覺，騎摩托車亦可以迷糊幾秒鐘。雖然他長期被疲累所困擾，但執起筆，就把疲累給忘了。

　　說起來也許有人不信，他寫作不分時間不選環境，有年暑假，他來往潮州與高雄之間的火車上，十二次搭車而振筆疾書，交出的成績是四十六首短詩！

他常說：「越忙越有時間。」這話有點怪，也的確有幾分歪理！因為忙才會把握時間珍惜時間，越閒越懶散，往往把許多時間浪擲。所以他那四十多首小詩，他一直認為是在百忙中給逼出來的。他不相信靈感，他覺得靈感不過是觀察、體驗、閱讀、思考的結果。所謂神來之筆，是長期思考與蘊釀的結晶。總之，勇於執筆是最重要的，有時儘管有許多寫作素材，不提筆只是空想而已。所以，他視寫作如惜命，所以，他寧願老家那四畝地兒荒廢，絕不放棄心田的耕耘！

1986 年 1 月 1 日屏東青年

按：本文作者為作家，本名朱章新，筆名朱煥文，擅寫小說，兼及小品，已故。

永遠用熱情執筆的詩人
── 許其正

林　野

　　除了我日常生活的實錄和心路歷程以外，多寫鄉土、大自然，歌頌人生的光明面，立足人道，勉人奮發向上向善……

　　我一向秉持這一理念，既為詩文，要發表，要感動讀者，引發共鳴，先須通情達意，讓讀者讀得懂……雖然詩重含蓄之美…但是仍願我的詩中意能讓你讀懂，從瞭解進而欣賞。

　　詩人許其正在「南方的一顆星」這本詩集的後記中寫下這些文字，他不僅告訴了大家，詩人自己的詩歌寫作方向，也點明了他的詩作風格，那就是熱忱、樸實、充滿向上的激情。

> 是誰在往上拋灑的呢？／他竟然有那麼奇妙
> 的神力／那一把把白色的細石子／經他往上一
> 拋灑／就綻放成了一叢叢白色的小花／一叢叢
> 純潔　一叢叢美

「噴泉」原本是樸實的，但在這首詩裡一下子成了
一個創造美，創造純潔的魔法師，它讓拋起的細石子（噴
泉水），一眨眼變成了一叢叢白色的小花，詩歌意象之
美，既充滿童趣的色彩又細膩輕鬆，字裡行間的緊嚴相
連，讓人讀之有形神豐美的感覺，恰如信筆神來。

立足人世，如果能給人向上向善的勵勉，那麼他的
人生無疑將是一個豐富、積極的人生。作為一個一生投
入在教育事業上的詩人，許其正是這樣一個飽含無限愛
心的詩人，他在「那螢火蟲」中所抒懷的恰恰是這種箴
言：

> 它帶給我一線光明，一線希望／也帶給我一陣
> 激勵，一陣鼓舞／更帶給我這樣的啓示／／在
> 任何惡劣的環境裡都該奮發向前／莫為自己
> 力量的渺小而自暴自棄／有一分能便出一分

力，發一線光

只有熱情向上的人生才是充滿希望的人生，誠如佛家所云，施者便是功德。就像我們有了愛心、有了奉獻就會有幸福的感覺一樣。

詩人很多時候不僅滿懷熱情，更是一個純淨不容污染的人，他們愛著這個世界、愛著大自然、愛著每一個有生命的事物。

　　小孩的臉是一座花園／形形色色的花／經常在這裡綻放／／引來許多眷顧／引來許多歡欣／引來許多讚美

兒童的心靈是最純淨的，就像這「小孩的臉」純淨得可以盛放各種各樣的花。同時孩子的心靈也是最脆弱的，所以詩人一邊為孩子們的純潔充滿嚮往和眷顧，又擔心這美好被人為地破壞，因此詩人感慨地希望著：

　　但願這一張臉／永遠繁花盛開／沒有風雨來干擾破壞

其實，詩歌無論怎麼寫，但最終的目的都是想讓讀者領悟、欣賞，如果一首詩，除了作者自己之外沒有一個讀者，我不知道這首詩的命運是什麼樣的結果。

詩人許其正的詩是樸實的，也是明朗的、健康的，更是熱情的、向善的，也因此感染了我，讓我忍不住寫下：

> 楊，我祈禱的福祉／起不了什麼作用／但是我希望／你腳下遺落的種子／在明年春天／會成為一片森林

我知道，祝福的話只能是一些文字，就像對《楊》，我更希望看到的是詩人的作品能成為更多的人指導希望的航船。

2001 年 5 月大海洋詩雜誌

按：本文作者為大陸名詩人，本名莊漢東，曾居浙江、新疆等地，失聯。

兩岸風光兩岸情

——讀許其正詩集《海峽兩岸遊蹤》

王式儉

　　台灣詩人許其正以現代田園詩見長。八十年代末，當我在藍海文先生選編的《當代台灣詩萃》（湖南文藝出版社一九八八）偶然讀到他那首膾炙人口的〈果樹園的呼喚〉時，曾深為詩中濃郁溫馨的田園詩情所感染。一九九五年，我有幸拜讀詩人寄自彼岸的新著詩集《南方的一顆星》，這部詩集，讓我又一次感受到詩人的田園情懷。集中許多詩作清新質樸，至今令我記憶猶新。如詩人懷念先母的〈詠母親〉，勉人勤奮的〈聞雞〉，感嘆時光易逝的〈蟬殼〉、〈金龜子〉，詩趣盎然的〈雨滴的舞蹈〉，富有哲思的〈鴿子〉、〈某鳥園遇雨〉等。許其正的詩多寫鄉土、大自然，歌頌人生光明面，勉人奮發，向真向善。正如伍澤元先生在〈序〉中所說：「許其正老師在〈南方的一顆星〉詩集中，表現出與鄉土、田園、大自然間的和諧，恬淡而平易近人，充滿人性光明面。」

近由北京團結出版社出版的許其正詩集《海峽兩岸遊蹤》（中英對照），是詩人近年往返海峽兩岸所寫旅遊詩的一部分，集中選詩四十八首，讓我領略到許其正詩歌的另一個側面。

旅遊詩又稱風景詩或山水詩。晉宋之際詩人謝靈運開中國山水詩風，後起之秀是謝朓，人稱「小謝」。在山水詩發展上，謝朓的貢獻尤大，唐代的王維、孟浩然等人的作品，頗受其影響。李白曾有「蓬萊文章建安骨，中間小謝又清發」的感慨。二謝為當時「淡乎寡味」的詩，輸入了新鮮的血液，對山水詩的盛行和玄言詩的消歇起到了積極的作用。山水詩易泥實、平泛，往往流於寫實性描寫，缺少意象的虛實變幻。許其正的山水風景詩觀察細膩，描寫逼真，避免了泥實、平泛。他的作品有許多傳神的刻劃和新穎的意境。詩人是這樣描寫台灣恆春半島「貓鼻頭」的景象的：**輕步來到海邊／那隻貓以捕獵之姿／慢移向前／／鼻尖快碰到海水了／他仍然慢移向前／向巴士海峽……**。詩中作者將「貓鼻頭」的奇景寫得活靈活現，其聲息、動態彷彿可聞可見。在這個集中，〈葡京大賭場〉意象也很新穎：**夕陽像一隻受驚嚇的夾尾狗／被夜驅逐追趕，快速逸去／從世界各**

地聚攏來的賭客們／便因心中貪婪的鼓動，紛紛／鑽進那隻大蝙蝠的雙翼下……。澳門葡京大賭場建築正像一隻展翅的大蝙蝠。賭客們從門口進入，正如鑽進它的雙翼下。詩人正是抓住了葡京賭場的這一形象特徵進行渲染，並表達自己的情緒的。

許其正的山水詩具有不同的風格與情調。不論是登山，還是臨水，作者都能用富於變化的筆繪聲繪影地描繪出彼時彼地的景物和風光，並能在徜徉山水中寄託自己的情懷。如在〈夏夜，灘江上〉，作者將夏夜比作一名撫琴輕吟淺唱的吟遊詩人，同樣採用擬人化手法描寫夏夜灘江上的「竹筏」和「遊艇」等。在組詩〈黃山掠影〉中，詩人將「猴子觀海」寫得十分傳神：蹲立峰頂／石猴張開手掌放在眉頭上／眺望前方／／身子左右微晃／努力搜尋著／他在眺望、搜尋什麼？／前方呀／陰時，多雲／晴時，太平（猴子觀海又名猴觀太平，太平指太平縣，安徽黃山市所轄。）詩中景語情語並用，一語雙關，耐人尋味。

在這部集子裡，〈我登上了長城〉、〈長江大橋〉、〈今人稱奇的地方〉、〈再見北斗七星〉等詩也很引人矚目。在這些詩中，流露出的強烈的民族意識和愛國情懷，是感人至深的。在〈我登上了長城〉中，詩人動情地寫道：我登上了長城，讓雙腳／踩踏在實實在在的階梯上／再怎麼用力踩踏都踏踏實實／不再有以往只看圖片／那種夢般疑真似幻的感覺……。在〈長江大橋〉中詩人是這樣讚美這座由中國人自建，世界最長的雙層橋樑的雄姿的：以鋼筋為骨水泥沙石為身／橫跨中國最大河流之上／再大的江水，再蠻橫的急湍亂流／都撼不動那些精壯的樁腳／都摧不毀那些堅定的意志／中國人的睿智和魄力誰能蔑視？……但詩人並未停留於對大橋的讚美，而想到人們心中的另一座有待築造的大橋，詩中感嘆道：「未雲何龍？未雨何虹？」／何其雄壯美觀有用的長江大橋／只是另一座長江大橋／要待哪些中國人來築造？／要到何時才能建成？〈令人稱奇的地方〉是寫盤錦這片昔日不見經傳的荒蕪不毛之地是如何突現奇蹟般變化，成為詩人眼前大廈林立、綠地千頃的。詩人感嘆道：何以怕鹹的香稻能在鹽鹹地生長？／何以荒蕪不毛能變興盛繁榮？／是誰將腐朽化為神奇？／是誰為她點化成今日模樣？……〈再見北斗七星〉是寫參加內蒙古海拉爾舉行的中國新文學學會第十六屆學術年會及草原之旅，是夜，詩人在湛藍的蒼穹中見到北斗七星的情景。在這首詩中，詩人筆下的大草原顯得那麼親切、寧靜和安祥！詩中寄託了詩人對祖國大陸的無限深情。詩中這樣寫道：那是北斗七星，依稀／我童年看見的模樣／／驚喜中，我深深地，貪婪地／吸著潔淨無塵的空氣，頓覺／四周盈滿許多熟悉之物：／我童年時鄉間的綠景、芬芳／以及鄉人樸素的語言笑貌／／我的整個身心沉浸在／愉悅和甜美的回憶中／一如和久別的老友重逢／在這異鄉的陌生草原……作者在〈序〉中說：自己早年雖然曾經因為暈車，不喜歡旅遊，但是從中年以後，卻由於各種因素，反而喜愛上了它，除了幾乎遊遍了出生地台灣，遊蹤也遍及中國大陸、日本、韓國、新加坡、泰國、印尼、加拿大、美國等地，並將持續延伸擴及其他國家或地區。詩人曾風趣地將自己的旅行比作一次次刺激驚險的「滑沙」，比作蒙古包內大嚼特嚼的「全羊大餐」。詩人寫道：長久被禁錮著／總在書頁間巡行諸多名勝古蹟／……一旦放行／便風馳電掣下滑／才聽風聲在耳邊颯颯而行／沒多久，輕舟已過萬重山／……正如這一行／最先落腳盤錦、瀋陽／而後山海關、北戴河／現在已在南戴河……在這本詩集中，詩人不止一次這樣描寫旅途的美景：一幅緊接著一幅／或遠，或近／或高，或低／處處美景／令人目不暇接／它們全部都是／一幅幅山水國畫……；詩人不能忘懷自己在旅途之中受到祖國同胞的殷勤款待和友好情誼；不能忘懷蒙古包內「那些豪放的熱情」；不能忘懷「把夜照得明亮如白晝」的篝火，和在「這旺燃著篝火和歌聲裡」把人們的熱血煮得沸沸揚揚的「熱舞」；不能忘懷在吐魯蕃隔鄰主人相贈的那串「每顆都鼓脹飽滿／泛溢著友情的芳香／包裹著友情瓊漿」的「好重好大的」葡萄……

　　山水有真賞，吟詠有真得。（明‧陳繼儒）許其正先生的山水詩表現出強烈的民族意識，以及詩中所表達出的對源遠流長的民族文化難以割捨的愛國熱情，給我留下了深刻印象。古人云：「凡士之蘊其所有」，常寄情於山水。望合厭分是兩岸同胞共同的心願，也是中華民族自有歷史以來歷代人的希望。許其正先生的詩集《海峽兩岸遊蹤》正是通過寄情山水來表達海峽兩岸同胞這一夙願的。

2003 年 11 月 8 日國際漢語詩壇
2003 年 11 月 15 日葡萄園詩刊
2003 年 12 月大海洋詩雜誌

　　按：本文作者為大陸名詩人，長住陝西西安，已故。

有情有畫談海峽兩岸遊蹤

王常新

　　讀了許其正先生的旅遊詩《海峽兩岸遊蹤》，我也像他一樣：「呼出喧囂，吸進幽靜／呼出枯黃，吸進翠綠／呼出厭煩，吸進愉悅／呼出市塵，吸進山林」（杉林溪）；這就因為他的詩有情有畫。

　　我們讀〈恆春半島速寫四首〉中的〈貓鼻頭〉，看到「*輕步來到海邊／那隻貓以捕獵之姿／慢移向前／鼻尖都快碰到海水了／他仍然慢移向前／向巴士海峽……*」。我們的眼前不是呈現一幅幅動畫麼！當我們再讀到「*似乎，魚的香味正誘引著他／似乎，他的眼睛已透視到了可口的魚／哇，他的鼻尖就要碰到海水了！*」我們的心中不也燃燒起火熱的激情麼！

　　「*熱情的海是一名藍衣武士／日夜期盼著和沙灘幽會／從遙遠的地方來／瘋狂地嘶吼著／猛奔而上……／海灘則是一名靜女／蘊蓄著的情意／綿密如*

細沙／期待著／海的奔赴……」（〈白沙灣〉）；湧動的海潮，靜臥的海灘，確實讓我想起，「靜女其姝」那浪漫的味道，也是有情有畫的好例。

在〈一串葡萄〉中，詩人吟道：「雙手幾乎難以捧起的／心間幾乎難以承接的／好重好大的／這一串葡萄！」我頓時感到這一串葡萄，「好重好大」。當我讀到以下的句子，「比翠玉更珍貴的／這一串葡萄／令我捧得手顫」／令我接得心動」，我馬上想起「桃花潭水深千尺，不及汪倫送我情」，詩人像李白一樣採用比物手法，既富有生動形象，又顯得情深意切。

〈一串葡萄〉歌頌了同胞的手足之情，〈令人稱奇的地方——盤錦印象〉則稱讚同胞改天換地，征服自然的偉跡：「何以怕鹹的香稻能在鹽鹹地生長？／何以荒蕪不毛能變興盛繁榮？／是誰將她點化成今日模樣的？／啊，那真是一個令人稱奇的地方！」這一連串的說詞和最後的驚嘆，充分表達了詩人對大陸同胞的敬佩之情。

在〈長江大橋〉中，詩人淋漓盡致地表現了深深的民族情：「再大的水，再蠻橫的急湍亂流／都撼不動那些粗壯的樁腳／都摧不毀那些堅定的意志／中國人的睿智和魄力誰能篾視？」在註中詩人又註明：「長江大橋由中國人自建，未依靠任何外力。」讀到這些，我們

不也和詩人一樣，澎湃起民族自豪感嗎！再讀到「只是
另一座長江大橋／要待哪些中國人來築造？要到何時
才能建成？」我也和詩人一樣，為海峽兩岸尚未統一而
唏噓不已。

〈我登上了長城〉則是發思古之幽情，詩人感嘆：
「我登上了長城，讓身子／前移在兩牆之間的階梯上／
再怎麼繼續前移都彷彿無止無盡／難以窮盡它們／那
萬里的長途跋涉……」詩人對我們的祖先所創造的聞名
世界的物質文明和精神文明發出由衷的禮讚。

詩人在抒發感情和繪製圖畫詩裡用了多種技巧，增
加了詩歌的魅力。

在〈青蛙石〉中，詩人吟道：「我似乎聽到了／噗
通噗通跳下水的聲音／和我小時候在水邊聽到的／一
模一樣」。這是通過幻聽，表現詩人陶醉在童年故事生
活的回憶中。詩人有異於常人的幻聽能力。他通過幻
覺，變異對象，創造出更高真實的假象。

在〈祝山日出即景〉中，詩人把雲和太陽寫活了：

都已經是什麼時代了
那些雲還那麼害羞
你瞧！她們只因為無意間看到太陽
洗完澡，從中央山脈東面

　　那個大澡盆裡，赤裸地站起來
　　就害羞得滿臉通紅，甚至羞紅到兩耳根
　　甚至羞紅遍整個脖子

　　詩人把人所具有的表情和動作加到雲和太陽上，讓我們看到一幅生動的圖畫，感受到詩人看到祝山日出的喜悅心情。

　　〈漓江舟泛〉吟道：「蟬鳴和鳥囀細雨般噴灑各處／增加清爽、寧靜和悠閒的強度／清風徐來，水波微漾／來出漾起臉上滿意的微笑」。在這裡，詩人將無形的聲音變為有形的細雨，給我們創造出陌生化的效果，讓我們感覺清新可喜。

　　〈哈爾濱小唱〉之〈豪情的城市〉吟道：「哇！這豪情的城市／我只被他輕輕一吻／便全身著火了！」在這裡，詩人反客為主，變被動為主動，表現出他到達豪情的城市後受到巨大的感染，自己也豪情萬丈起來了。

　　〈張家界，詩三首〉中的〈十里畫廊寫真〉首節與末節用了圖像詩的形式來表現十里畫廊的面貌。

　　首節是：
　　一幅
　　　緊
　　　　接

著
一幅

末節是：
一幅
緊接著
一
幅

　在這裡，詩人依靠文字排列或變化，描繪張家界十里畫廊景點的形狀。首節的排列使我們感到在觀賞一幅幅畫，它的裝裱形制是橫卷，而且是其中的長卷；末節的排列，則讓我們看到橫卷之後，緊接著是直幅形式的立軸。這樣精心的安排，就讓我們感受到這一景點中山的雄奇和霧的縹緲，令人目不暇接。這也是「詩中有畫」傳統的創新。

　《海峽兩岸遊蹤》可稱道之處尚有許多，如詩人對世事的關懷，見諸於〈葡京大賭場〉、〈祝山日出即景〉等詩，高尚的情操見諸於〈詩贈沙漠三傑〉〈在寒山寺〉等詩，擅長用呼告語和省略號描寫洶湧浪潮的〈觀錢塘潮〉一詩，因篇幅所限，就不贅述了。

2003 年 12 月大海洋詩雜誌
2004 年 5 月 8 日世界詩人信使

　按：本文作者為大陸名詩人，武漢華中師大教授。

和炎夏分享綠蔭的清涼

—— 許其正中英對照詩集《胎記》片論

王式儉

　　在台灣詩人中，許其正是很有特色的一位。他一直立足人道，寫鄉土、田園，歌頌自然和人生，勉人奮發向善。詩人從上世紀六十年代開始發表新詩和散文作品，已出版《半天鳥》等 5 部新詩集及《毯苗》等 6 部散文集，作品被譯成英、日、希臘、蒙古國等外國文字，入選十數種選集。新近由國際詩歌翻譯研究中心和環球出版社聯合出版的詩集《胎記》，收入詩人近十餘年來部分詩作 54 首。從這本裝幀精美的詩集中，我們欣喜地看到詩人的視野又有了新的拓展。他的詩變得更為深沉、厚重，更加注重精神的內斂。從他一些詩中，透露出詩人對現代都市生活的憂慮不安和對社會民生的關注。

　　在這本詩集中，值得關注的是詩人反映都市生活的一些篇什。在《陰陽界》中，詩人寫道：“那是什麼地方？／是陰間還是人寰？／蒼蒼莽莽之間／只見一幢幢／大大小小的建物／／向東看是如此／向西看是如此／向南北看是如此／……／／我站在這裡／不知道所看到的／哪個方位是墳塋／哪個方位是屋宇？……”在詩的末尾感嘆道：“這裡可是陰陽的分界？／我迷惑不知呀迷惑不知／……”面對灰色的世界，都市大大小小的水泥建築，詩人感到人生的迷惘和困惑。在〈獨〉這首詩中，詩人目光關注的是“在街廊的一個角落”的一位“孤獨老人”，表達出對這位老人深深的同情。詩中寫道：“坐在地上／靠牆瞌睡著／孤寂將他緊緊裹住／／人潮波湧，熙熙攘攘／車流奔逐，匆匆而過／／他坐在地上／靠牆瞌睡著／誰都沒有理睬／只有落塵飄落／只有他自己……”這兩首詩，前者寫在1996年8月，後者寫於1997年7月，兩首詩放在一起，無形中形成一種極大的反差，一邊是高樓林立，一邊卻是孤獨的老人棲身街頭，無有立足之地。尤其令人痛心的是人們麻木不仁，無人理會，揭示出現代社會生活人與人之間的冷漠和社會生活極不和諧的現狀。在另一首題為「塞車」的詩中，詩人無奈地寫道：“……前後左右都是／車輛、車輛、車輛……烏煙瘴氣、烏煙瘴氣……／／我要怎麼走呢？／好像被困在迷魂陣裡／總覺得處處有險阻、陷阱／……”尤其讓詩人感到無奈的是，在這些車陣中，卻仍有人不依規矩，強佔，搶位……在〈暈〉中，詩人疑惑道：“在公車上／怎麼像在船上？／／……地球是一艘船／還是一輛公車？／／在人生旅途上／我現在身在何處？”此外，詩人在〈行道樹〉、〈從砂場邊走過〉、〈無力感〉等詩中，對山林被“濫墾濫伐”，鮮綠被水泥叢林“鯨吞”，以及新新人類的“做惡、懶散、奢侈”表現出極大的憂慮和憤慨。詩人認為：一個人“做惡多端”，往往會迷失自己。他在〈藏鏡一說〉中這樣描繪那位“藏鏡人”，詩中寫道：“我是誰？”／“我到底是誰？”／那個人狂喊著／在布袋戲舞台上／在迷蒙的塵世間／你困惑地說／……

　　中國近代著名的美學家王國維在《人間詞話》中說：“詞以境界為最上，有境界則自成高格。”他說：“境非獨謂景物也。喜怒哀樂，亦人心中之一境界。故能寫真景物、真感情者，謂之有境界。”王國維認為嚴羽所說的“妙悟”、“別趣”和王世慎所說的“神韻”，只不過說明了現象，而有境界才是詩歌審美創作的根本。他說：“詩有題而詩亡，詞有題而詞亡。”“詩詞之題目本為自然及人生。”認為，文學應以自然及人生為題材，表現對自然人生之領悟。他曾明確提出境界創造的藝術要求。他說：“何以謂之有境界？”曰：“寫情則沁人心脾，寫景則在人耳目，述事則如其口出是也。"並說："大家之作，其言情也必沁人心脾，其寫景也必豁人耳目。其辭脫口而出，無矯揉裝束之態，以其所見者真，所知者深也，詩詞皆然。持此以衡古今之作者，可無大誤矣；王國維曾說："詞人者，不失其赤子之心者也。"赤子即嬰兒，所謂"赤子之心"即"童心"。他唱導的不失赤子之心者，能寫真景物真感情者，正是針對清末虛偽、腐朽的社會風氣而言的。以許其正先生近年發表的一些詩作，如〈中國結〉、〈紅尾伯勞的哀訴〉、〈鴿子與戰士〉等，我們不時可以看到詩人這種赤子情懷以及對民族文化的熟稔和鍾愛。在〈紅尾伯勞的哀訴〉中，詩人對弱者寄予了深深的同情。伯勞，又名鵙，是古書上就歌詠的一種鳥。《詩經》云："七月鳴鵙，八月載績。"意思是說，七月伯勞鳴叫，八月績麻。這首詩以陷入鳥仔踏中一隻無辜伯勞的口吻，訴說了這不幸的遭遇。詩中寫道："嘎嘎，我陷在人類鳥仔踏的陷阱裡了／我展翅欲飛，卻為繩索所縛，吊在半空中／我呼天搶地，喊破喉嚨，也是徒然／當飛得倦了，捕捉害蟲累了／我站在孤枝頂上休息到底犯了什麼罪？／……"在詩的末尾，這隻無辜的益鳥絕望地叫喊："人類呀，嘎嘎，你們的良心何在？／嘎嘎，如何才能喚醒你們的良心？"這首詩在手法上僅採用了擬人和反復，語言完全採用口語；但詩中這隻益鳥的無辜無助和它撕裂心脾的呼喊，卻能打動讀者。〈鴿子和戰士〉一詩寫於 1997 年 8 月漢城（現今首爾）戰爭紀念館，表達了詩人對戰爭的憎惡和對和平生活的祈願。這首詩語言親切平和、精煉，情感真摯，意象鮮明，可謂許先生近年詩歌創作的翹楚。

　　許其正所著詩集《胎記》中還有許多詩值得我們精讀和品味。這些詩構思十分新穎，兼具田園和都市，揉合了鄉土、自然和詩人的智慧。如〈熨〉、〈腳印・踩在沙灘上〉、〈玩沙者〉、〈我看見了時光〉、〈回首〉、〈誰曾打敗過時光〉等，在這些詩中，或自況，或諷喻，或靈視，無不寄託作者對人生的感悟和對童稚時代的追懷。捧讀許其正的詩集《胎記》，正值炎夏，這自然讓我想起這位詩人早年的成名詩作〈果樹園的呼喚〉中沁人心脾的詩句，使我彷彿置身於詩人辛勤經營的果香四溢的果園，讓人忘卻夏日的燠熱和疲倦。在這裡，可以領略到成熟豐碩之美，可以和詩人分享綠蔭的清涼和創作的甘甜！

　　　　　　　　　　　2006 年 8 月 8 日世界詩人

許其正的詩初探

扎洛尼

這是我首次覺得有必要並樂於"談論"一個遙遠國度的外國詩人即中國台灣許其正的詩。

這位中國詩人的靈感來自大自然、海洋，樹林，並受陽光撫吻而綻放。

他用生命的彩筆寫出偉大的詩篇，欣然展翅向前「飛翔」……

許其正伴隨著他的詩一起上升，以提升他的生命。我為這位中國詩人所寫的深湛詩意而驚愕瞠目，尤其題為"根"這首詩。根……伸展著，探索著，深入著……。

他讓他的想像，緊緊盯著海，來創造意象，溢出美感，並觀賞南方的一顆星在滄海的上空閃爍，築出無數的橋與我們溝通。他還傳遞出他的微笑和希冀。多麼偉大的心靈呀，許其正的心靈！

他的詩有時轉到他的童年、青年和壯年。他頗具才華，也以其極大的體貼詠頌他的母親。春天來時，他則用詩來予以詮釋。中國詩人許其正引我敬重並讚賞中國人民和詩人。（國詩歌翻譯研究中心）

2006 年 6 月大海洋詩雜誌
2006 年 8 月 8 日世界詩人

按：本文作者為希臘扎洛尼文學會會長，擅詩畫，其夫安東尼擅翻譯，兩人相搭配，她因年紀大，被稱祖母詩人。

Hsu ChiCheng: "Birthmark", Poems

Zacharoula Gaitanaki

"On the grass and flowers in the field
A dewdrop
Crystal-clear and sparkling

What does it expect else?
Doesn't it know all beautiful things
Always disappear rapidly?"

("Morning Dew",P.80)

I read with much interest every poem that Mr. Hsu ChiCheng wrote (in his poetic collection "Birthmark") and find that he is a talented and famous poet. The creation of a new world, with peace, sincerity, beauty, love, flowers, etc., isn't only a poet's dream. It's a feasible target.

Honesty, humanity, peace, nature, life, sound, the

wind, the countryside, clouds, wings became verses, poems, songs… His poetry is like "The eternal spring", "The wind of the time", "The flowers of the sound", "A mountain path". It's like "An image of the time", "Flame in winter", "Morning Dew" and "Birthmark". The poet "Spreading the wings" give us a fine collection of poetry.

I find Mr. Hsu ChiCheng's poems very readable. Read his tasteful book. It's worth it.

許其正詩集《胎記》簡評

扎卡勞娜・蓋坦納克

"在田野的花草上
朝露，顆顆綻放
晶瑩剔透

它還在期待什麼？
所有美麗的東西不是
很快就會消失的嗎？"

　　我滿懷興致品讀完許其正先生的詩集《胎記》中的每一首詩。我知道他是一個多才多藝且聞名遐邇的詩人。他以和平、真誠、美、愛、花等，所構築的新世界，不是一個夢想。而是一個可以抵達的目標。

　　正義、人性、和平、大自然、生命、聲音、風、鄉間、雲朵、翅膀都成了他的詩句、詩篇和歌……他的詩像"永恆的春天"、"時光的風"、"聲音之花"、"山路"。有如"時間的影像"、"冬天裡的紅火"、"朝露"和"胎記"。詩人"展開翅膀"，為我們奉獻出一部優秀的詩集。

　　我以為，許其正先生的詩可讀性極高。他雅致的詩集頗具欣賞價值。（張智譯）

　　　　　　　　2006 年 8 月 8 日世界詩人

　按：作者為希臘著名女詩人，翻譯家及評論家。

BIRTHMARK, Poems　　by Hsu ChiCheng

Φορτωμένος τιμαλφή υλικά, εξορυγμένα από τον εσωτερικό του κόσμο περπατάει στις ακρώρειες του καλού λόγου, παλεύει την καρδιά και το αίμα του κάθε ποιήματός του. Φως εκ φωτός αναδύεται. Εμείς ψαρεύουμε μαργαριτάρια που τα κύματα των εμπνεύσεών του κουβαλούν μέσα σε όστρακα του Ειρηνικού ωκεανού... Ναι φίλοι, αναγνώστες ως την μακρινή Taiwan φθάνει ο Έλληνας ποιητής για ν' αλιεύσει μαργαριτάρια.

Η θάλασσα είναι μια *«ηρωίδα»*, *«Η θάλασσα είναι μια χορεύτρια».* Τρομάζει βλέποντας τις πτυχές στο σώμα του... Όχι όμως στην ψυχή του. Η ψυχή του ποιητή πάντα μένει άνθος θαλερό. *«Πτυχές, οι πτυχές στα ρούχα, πτυχές, οι πτυχές στο μέτωπό της, πτυχές, οι πτυχές της ζωής».*

«Πρέπει να αφήσω να παραμείνουν τα ίχνη των ποδιών μου». Ναι, ποιητή... Hsu Chi Cheng. Θ' αφήσεις τα ίχνη σου και στις δικές μας θάλασσες και με πτυχές στο σάρκινο ρούχο σου, θα γράψεις πολλά ποιήματα ακόμη αφήνοντας έτσι τα ίχνη σου στη ζωή.

«Στο ταξίδι της ζωής, που είμαι τώρα;» Μακρύ ας είναι ακόμη το ταξίδι σου.

Σου το εύχομαι...

Μη σε τρομάζει ο χρόνος.

Τρέχει γρήγορα , ε και; Αφήνει πίσω τη νιότη μας με τα λαμπερά μάτια, το λαμπερό δέρμα. Τα αχνά άσπρα μας δόντια. Αχ! χρόνε, γιατί δεν μας γυρίζεις λίγο πίσω; Κι εγώ κι εσύ κι όλοι οι ποιητές που 'χουμε ανάγκη από πολύ χρόνο για να γεμίσουμε τα όστρακα μαργαριτάρια ν' αλιεύουν οι άνθρωποι που αγαπούν κι επιθυμούν την πνευματική ανάταση κι ευδαιμονία.

Και...

«Επειδή ήμασταν παιδιά και μικρά παιδιά τότε

η άνοιξη πάντοτε διαπερνούσε τα σώματά μας

Οποτεδήποτε ανακαλώντας την παιδική μας ηλικία

ακόμη τα άσπρα μου μακριά μαλλιά να γυρίσουν ξανά

η αμυδρή όρασή μου θέλει ξανά να γίνει καθαρή».

Την αιώνια Άνοιξη επιθυμείς ποιητή.

Σε τούτη την ποιητική συλλογή, που σου μεταφράσαμε, ζωηρά αναπολείς τη νιότη σου. Και ποιος δεν την αναπολεί... Ο ουρανός ήταν τότε πιο καθαρός και η αύρα απαλή χωρίς αμφιβολία... και προπαντός δεν φοβόμαστε...

Ωραία είναι η ζωή λέμε εμείς οι Έλληνες κι ας μην βλέπουμε με τα κουρασμένα πια μάτια μας, την τόση ομορφιά. Την αισθανόμαστε. Είμαστε ποιητές... Έχουμε εντός μας τα πιο λαμπερά μάτια και το πιο αρυτίδωτο πρόσωπο. Είμαστε έφηβοι. Πάντα έφηβοι.

Παναγιώτα Ζαλώνη

Λογοτέχνης

Πρόεδρος του Λογοτεχνικού Ομίλου «ΖΑΛΩΝΗ» «΄ξάστερον»,

Εκδότρια του Λογοτεχνικού Περιοδικού,

Λόγου, Τέχνης και Πολιτισμού «ΚΕΛΑΙΝΩ»

Σεπτέμβριος 15, 2006

A literary approach by Mrs. Panagiota Zaloni,

Poetess, prose writer, treatise writer, painter, painter

of Holy Icons

Birthmark, Poems by Hsu ChiCheng

Panagiota Zaloni

Loaded with precious materials, plucked out from his interior world is walking in the tops of the good speech, he is smelting the heart and blood in each of his poem, light from light emerges. We picked up diamonds from the waves of his inspirations which carry into the shells of the Pacific Ocean…Yes, my reader friends up to the remote Taiwan, the Hellenic poet arrives in order to fish and collect diamonds.

The sea is a "**hero**", "**The sea is a dancer**". He is terrified seeing the wrinkles in his body…but not in his soul. The soul of poet ever remains a youthful bloom. "**Folds, the folds on the clothes,／Folds, the folds on his forehead,／Folds, the folds of life.**"" **I must let my footmarks remain!**" yet, poet…Hsu ChiCheng. You will leave your footmarks and to our seas and with wrinkles to your flesh clothe, you will write many poems yet, leaving your tracks in the life.

" In the journey of life, where I am now?" May it be long yet your life journey!

I wish you it to you.

Not be frightened by time. It is running so fast, and so? It is leaving back our youth with the bright eyes, the bright skin, our dim white teeth. Oh! Time, why you do not return back to us for few moments. And me and you and all the poets that we need so many time to fill the shells with diamonds to fish people who love and wish the spiritual exaltation and prosperity.

> "Because we were children and kits then
> Spring always dwelled in our clothes
> Whenever recalling my childhood
> Even my white hair longs to remain again
> My dim eyesight wants to clear again. "

The eternal Spring you desires poet.

In this poetic collection, what we have translated for

you, lively you recall your youth. And who does not recall same… The sky was then clearer and breeze smooth without doubt…and above all we are not afraid…

The life is beautiful we are saying us the Greeks(Hellenics) and we wish our tired now eyes that so much beauty. We feel same. We are poets… We have inside us the brightest eyes and the most wrinkleless face. We are adolescents. All times adolescents.

許其正詩集《胎記》管窺

扎洛尼

　　攜帶著珍貴的資材，往返於內心世界，他以高妙的語言提煉出他的心血，熔入他的每一首詩而光芒四射。我們從那源自太平洋貝殼裡的靈感之波裡採拾鑽石……。是的，我的讀者朋友，到台灣去吧，我們希臘詩人可去垂釣和搜集鑽石。

　　海是一個"英雄"，"海是一個舞者"。他為目睹他身體的皺褶而驚懼……但內心靈則說不。詩人的內心開滿青春之花。"皺褶，衣服的皺褶，／皺褶，額頭的皺褶／皺褶，人世的皺褶"。"我一定要留下腳印來！"是的，詩人……許其正。你將在我們的人世之海留下足跡，留下皺褶在你的軀殼上，而你將寫出大量的詩，在人世間留下你的履痕。

"在人生旅途上，／我身在何處？"你的人生該還悠長邈遠！

但願如此。

別為歲月所震懾。它跑得那麼快。是吧？它逃離我們的青春和明眸、潤膚、皓齒。啊！歲月，你為什麼不肯為我們回首逗留一會？我和你及所有詩人需要許多時光用鑽石把貝殼填滿，把魚獻給那些喜愛並企望心靈輝煌升華的人們。

而且

　　"因為那時我們是童稚
　　　身上棲居的是永遠的春天
　　　即使現在想起或有人提及
　　　稀疏的白髮都要急急回復濃黑
　　　茫茫的視力都要急急回復清明"

詩人呀！你希冀青春永駐。

在我們翻譯的這部詩集中，可讓你回憶起你鮮活的青春。誰沒有相同的回憶呢？……不可置疑，穹蒼更加清明了，微風輕輕吹拂著……。總之，我們坦蕩無懼……。

正如我們希臘人所言，生命是美麗的，而我們希冀用我們疲倦的眼睛看到它美麗如斯。我們有相同的感覺。我們都是詩人……。我們的內心擁有我們最明亮的眼睛和最沒皺褶的臉。我們依然年輕。時光永在。（野鬼譯）

2006 年 11 月 8 日世界詩人

按：本文為許其正中希對照詩集「胎記」的序文，刊印於該詩集第 6 至 11 頁，分別為希、英、中文。該詩集譯者為其夫銀行家、翻譯家安東尼（Antonios Zanolis）。迄本詩集出版的 2007 年 8 月為止，他已將英文、法文及義大利文文本譯為希臘文，出版 21 本書。

Literary Notes on Birthmark by Hsu ChiCheng

John Francis Missett

Today we are honoured to review the book of poetry. "Birthmark", written by the Great International and Chinese Poet Hsu ChiCheng of Taiwan. He is a native of Pingdong County Taiwan and we are sure that they are very proud of him there.

Editor, journalist, military judge, teacher and time education director. He is also a leading light in the mass organization of art and literature. He is now retired after thirty three years teaching.

He is becoming as well known in Greece and Brazil as he is in Taiwan and his poetry is sought after in China by *The World Poets Quarterly* of which body he is an adviser and his poetry featured in every issue.

This book opens with "Here". A simple poem of 4×4 lines and verses and whether the author means "raging" or "ragging". The poem holds together well. Winds rage and rag sail especially in the Eastern latitudes.

The second poem. "The Sea's five Appearances." Is technically wonderful. I who followed The sea for eleven years have not done as well .   Bravo Mr. Hsu.

Poem 3. Even in " Ironing". Nothing escapes the painter's eye of Mr. Hsu.

Poem 4. "Connecting a Wall in the mind". Scratch a poet's underneath is a Philosopher waiting to get out. Such a Philosopher too.

Poem5. "Footmarks on a sandy beach." Is a dialogue twixt the sane and the persistent. It works well.

Poem 6. "Carsickness". I love this poem. Although I have felt it many times I have never attempted to put it into words. Bravo Mr. Hsu.

Poem7. "A Wild Grass's account in its Own Words." The grass speaks and we grow wiser.

Poem8. "The Image of the Time". Mr. Hsu proves that though invisible Time does exist.

Poem9. "The Chinese Knot of the Time". There is a nice cultural parallel here with the story of Greece's Gordian knot, famously dealt with by Alexander The Great.

Bravo Mr. Hsu.

Poem10. "The place were the Human and Nether World meet". Hsu takes us to that point where reality and the intangible but real, meet.

Poem11. "I am Sorry Sir". This is a qualified apology as only an oriental could apologize. Bravo Mr. Hsu.

Poem12. "To Years." We are reminded how years gallop by as we long to return to hope.

Poem13. "Flames in winter." Winter in all of her cold glory shot through with flames of youth.

Poem14. "Wrinkles." Time whistles by and wrinkles, a hash look at old are. Old age can be harsh.

Poem 15. "I see time." A humourous look at time.

Poem16. "The Eternal Spring." The desire to return to youth and childhood and to stay there.

Poem17. "Loneliness." Here Hsu capitalizes on the loneliness of another and turns it into art.

Poem18. " The Literary Sketch about the Spring Field." This is a reverie about life and growth. Very pretty Mr. Hsu.

Poem19. "Reading a Letter." This is of course a love letter. This reveals to us here The West that The Chinese are romantically inclined.

Poem20. "Waterfall." Keeps up this theme. Even waterfall have love affairs in China.

Poem21. "One Who Plays with Fine Sand." Here the poet gives us a reverie using only fine sand to provoke our thought. Charming Mr. Hsu.

Poem 22. The poem "Powerless Sense." Is pure wisdom. Bravo Mr. Hsu.

Poem23. "The Lost sound." Proof that lost sounds are as important as "Lost Chords."

Poem24. "Sight Seeing." From China's Great Summer palace to the great Thunder Pagoda. (recently rebuilt) The poet mourns the lost atmospheres. Lovely bit of nostalgia.

Poem25. "The Waltz of the White Clouds." White Clouds, White Fogs, White Doves and waltz blending but never colliding.

Poem26. "Extempore Verse after Retirement." This is a shy look at retirement.

Poem27. "Birthmark." Is this book's title. Mr. Hsu reminds us that can't be cured must be endued.

Poem28. "Maple Leaves." Oh those wicked made up maple leaves.

Poem29. "The Flowers of Sound." The poet cleverly proves that the ear is the eye of the nighttime.

Poem30. "Flying." I am amazed. Everyone in China wishes to fly ...

Poem 31. The Poem Morning Dew is as Fresh and refreshing as The Morning Dew.

Poem32. "Willing." The poet shows as that the nicest sentiment is to wish others well.

Poem33. Old ages Speckles. "There are the foot-prints of time upon our flesh."

Poem34. "The Wind of the Time." Still on the theme of old age it is observed upon and well written up.

Poem35. "Looking Back." Still in the depths of Old Age The Poet risks a look back. Very nice Mr. Hsu.

Poem 36. "The roadside Trees." Who else but Hsu ChiCheng would notice and capitalize upon Roadside Tree's? Nice poem Mr. Hsu.

Poem37. "Hiding the Mirror." This is a poem about a person who has lost his mirror. Therefore he has no image to. Sad.

Poem38. "Going to the Countryside." The poet's wanderlust urges him out into the country. Inspiring poem,

In the poem "They are Still Alive." Number 39. Hsu ChiCheng reveals a tale of tragic everyday heroism. Two people by their unselfish acts allow two children to be saved at the cost of their own lives. Tearfully moving.

Poem40. Reading historical records. The Poet return to history for his theme...Bravo Mr. Hsu.

Poem 41. "Mythologies collapsing." The Poet takes on an angry bone with myth. Myths are important. History becomes legend. Legend becomes Myth. Myth becomes Psychology. If you get the history and myth wrong then the future psychology becomes flawed. A very sound observation Mr. Hsu.

Poem 42. " My Afternoon Mood." Mr. Hsu plunges into a plethora of questions which plague the elderly.

Poem43. "Traffic Jam's." Gently the poet reminds us of China's prosperity, when I was in China last everybody desired a bicycle and the sight of a car was an event.

Poem44. "Touching an Old scar." The Poet looks at an old scar, symbolic of the unhealed scars within his psyche and desires closure and there is none to be had.

Poem45. "The Mountain Path." Another beautiful walk with Hsu along Mountain Path. Excellent.

Poem46. "Flowers are Dancing Wildly." Hsu's flowers are all females in brightly coloured dresses of course. He even invites us to join in the dancing. This is fun.

Poem47. S.A.R.S.Saliva. This is a stern poem, a warning against the spread of S.A.R.S.

Poem 48. continues in this vein. "Saliva Quarantine" could well used by any Health Organization to promote a campaign against spiting. Very worthwhile.

In poem49 Hsu pokes a little fun at himself and his "Local Accent". Very Funny Mr. Hsu.

Poem50. "Returning". This poem makes you feel like you are in a railway carriage with the station zipping by as you head for home.

Poem51. The Poet asks. "Who , Even Once Has defeated time?" who has done this? Julius Ceasar? Alexander The Great? Genghis Khan? No- one.

Poem52. "Spreading the Wing." The poet's uncaged soul takes flight.

Poem 53. "Backbone." Here Hsu impartially praises The Hero and damns. The Coward with equal impartiality.

In his final poem in the excellent book. "Passing by a

Placer Deposit." The Poet's Soul within Hsu ChiCheng cries out for a return to nature sure and sweet ways, we can do nothing but agree with this sensitive soul and mourn out slowness to save out planet. Hsu ChiCheng I salute and embrace you for the poet you are. This book contains the finest of your poetry I have yet read. Bravo my learned friend.

許其正詩集《胎記》漫筆

〔英國〕約翰·弗朗西斯·米塞特

今天，我有幸閱讀並賞析由楊宗澤先生英譯的中國當代著名詩人許其正先生的詩集《胎記》。許先生生於台灣屏東縣；顯然，對於他的鄉人來說，許先生無疑是他們的自豪。

許先生曾從事過編輯、記者、軍法官和教師等職業，另兼多家文學社團的理事、顧問等職；從教三十三年後退休。

許先生的詩在國外特別是希臘、巴西等國如同在台灣一樣深有影響。他是《世界詩人》詩歌季刊的特約總編，幾乎每期刊物都刊發他的詩作；他的詩在中國有著眾多的讀者。

《胎記》一書的開山之篇是〈在這裡〉。由於作者把握得當，使得這首每節四句、共四小節的短詩像風鼓桅帆一樣回蕩在東方大地上。

詩作之二〈海的五貌〉技藝嫻熟，精彩得當。我曾在海上漂泊達十一年之久，卻未能寫出這般美的詩句。許先生，你真是太棒了！

詩作之三〈熨〉。即使在熨平生命之皺紋時，一切都逃不過詩人那雙畫家般的眼睛。

詩作之四〈牆的聯想〉。在牆上胡亂寫畫的詩人其實是一位俟機出道的哲人。許先生也正是那樣的一位哲人。

詩作之五〈腳印‧踩在沙灘上〉，是詩人與一位執著的追求者的詩性對話，寫得很成功。

詩作之六〈暈〉，寫得很不錯，我很喜歡。我一再地玩味，企圖把握其內蘊，而不是單純地望文生義。真有你的，你寫出這般好的詩！

詩作之七〈野草的自訴〉。聽著野草的訴說，我們變得聰明了起來。

詩作之八〈時間的影像〉。許先生用詩句證實時間也是一種存在。

　　詩作之九〈中國結 外解〉堪稱一首寫希臘故事中的偉人亞歷山大用快刀斬亂麻般的方式所解決的那個"難以解決的死結"具有同等文化意義的佳作。祝賀你啊，許先生！

　　詩作之十〈陰陽界〉，將我們帶到了一個現實世界與一個無形的、但很真實的世界的交界處。

　　詩作之十一〈對不起，老師〉表達了一種似乎只有東方人認可的道歉。好啊！許先生！

　　詩作之十二〈給歲月〉，讓我們想到，當我們渴望成功與希望的時候，時光則在不停地悄悄流失。

　　詩作之十三〈冬天裡的紅火〉，讓我們看到，冬日的嚴寒，被青春的火燄擊碎。

　　詩作之十四〈皺紋〉。時間呼嘯而過，我們的臉上長出皺紋，老去的歲月之聲對於老者來說格外刺耳。

　　詩作之十五〈我看見時光〉是對於時間的頗富幽默感的審視。

　　詩作之十六〈永遠的春天〉折射了詩人渴望回歸青少年時代的夢。

　　詩作之十七〈獨〉。在這首詩裡，詩人巧妙地將他人的孤獨與寂寞轉化為藝術。

　　詩作之十八〈春野速寫〉 是一曲人生與成長的幻

想曲，寫得很美。

詩作之十九〈讀信〉。顯然那是一封情書；它向我們表明：無論西方人還是中國人都是具有浪漫情懷的。

詩作之二十〈瀑布〉向我們展示了這樣一個主題：在中國，連瀑布都與愛有關。

詩作之二十一〈玩沙者〉。在這首詩裡，詩人通過玩細沙激發我們思想的夢幻。真了不起啊，許先生。

詩作二十二〈無力感〉充滿了智慧。感謝許先生為我們寫出這樣的好詩。

詩作二十三〈聲音迷蹤〉 向我們表明：失落的聲音就是"失落的心弦"。

詩作二十四〈遊覽〉寫了中國兩大古建築頤和園與雷鋒塔（新近重建），著重抒發了詩人為失去的藝術氛圍而悲哀的心緒，有懷舊之況味。

詩二十五〈白雲圓舞曲〉裡，白色的雲，白色的霧，白色的鴿子都百折不撓地飛翔、旋轉。

詩作二十六〈退休即興〉折射了詩人退休後的無奈心態。

詩作二十七〈胎記〉，該詩的題目是本詩集的名字，乃壓軸之作。它讓我不無偏頗地聯想起"既來之，則安之"的中國古訓。

詩作二十八〈楓葉〉——啊，那些調皮的楓葉啊！

　　詩作二十九〈聲音之花〉──詩人別具匠心地向我們昭示：耳朵是夜晚的眼睛。

　　詩作三十〈飛翔〉讓我們感到驚愕不已：每個中國人都渴望飛翔。

　　詩作三十一〈朝露〉裡詩之露珠如同朝露一樣清新、閃爍。

　　詩作三十二〈甘願〉　向我們展示了詩人最美好的情感，這就是：願妳活得比我好。

　　詩作三十三〈老人斑〉──老人斑是時間在我們的肌膚上留下的腳印。

　　詩作三十四〈時光的風〉也是一首寫老年人的詩。該詩觀察細膩，形容貼切，且述之極完備。

　　詩作三十五〈回首〉還是一首關於老年人的詩。詩人“不惜冒險”般地對於走過的人生之路進行了回顧。許先生，你寫得太美了。

　　詩作三十六〈行道樹〉──除了作為詩人的許先生，還有誰會留心路邊的樹木並將它們寫進詩裡呢？太棒了！

　　詩作三十七〈藏鏡一說〉，這首詩揭示了一個人無鏡可鑑的悲哀。

　　詩作三十八〈走向田園〉，詩人的漫遊癖促使他走出城市，走向農村，走進田園，確是一首鼓舞人心的好詩。

詩作三十九〈他們還活著〉 ，詩人向我們講述了一個頗具傳奇色彩的悲壯故事：在一場大地震中，兩個小孩子在他們的父母的懷抱中躲過了死神，他們的父母以自己的死換來了孩子的生，讀來感人之至。

詩作四十〈翻開歷史書頁〉一詩裡，詩人在史書裡找到了詩歌寫作的主題。祝賀你，許先生。

詩作四十一〈神話崩坍〉，在這首詩裡，詩人給神話以憤怒抨擊。神話固然重要，但歷史變成傳說，傳說變成神話，神話變成人的心態。這首詩告訴我們：如果你把歷史與神話顛倒，世人的心態就會出現瑕疵。確是一首富於洞察力的好詩。

詩作之四十二〈午後心情〉，在這裡，詩人陷於一種迷憒；這種迷憒對於中老年人來說是一種心靈和精神上的折磨。

詩作之四十三〈塞車〉，這首詩讓我想起了中國目前的繁榮與昌盛。當我在中國的時候，人人都渴望擁有一輛自行車，那時候，看見一輛汽車似乎都是一件很榮幸的事。

詩作之四十四〈碰觸舊創〉——人們在看一處飽含精神傷痛、尚未癒合的象徵性的傷疤；而這一傷疤是其他人們所沒有的。

　　詩作之四十五〈山路〉寫得很精彩，堪稱許先生沿著山間小道的一次美麗的漫步。

　　詩作之四十六〈花正飛舞〉，在這首詩裡，許先生筆下的花朵都是雌性的，自然也打扮得五彩繽紛；許先生似乎在用詩向我們發出邀請，請我們加入花之舞中，真是有趣得很。

　　詩作之四十七〈SARS·口水〉是一首主題嚴肅的詩作，是警惕 SARS 病毒傳播蔓延的警告。

　　詩作之四十八〈口水·隔離〉甚至可以用作衛生行政機構動員民眾不要隨地吐痰的動員令，極富社會意義。

　　詩作之四十九〈鄉音〉，在這首詩裡，詩人對於自己的鄉音做了頗有幽默色彩的揶揄，很有意思。

　　詩作五十〈歸〉，讀後，你會有一種好像坐在火車裡朝家的方向奔馳時飛速經過每一個車站時的感覺。

　　詩作五十一〈誰曾打敗過時光〉，在這首詩裡，詩人不斷地發問，"誰曾打敗過時光？"是凱撒大帝？是偉大的亞歷山大？還是不可一世的成吉思汗？回答顯然是否定的；沒有人能夠打敗時光！也沒有人曾經打敗過時光！

　　詩作五十二〈展開翅膀〉，是詩人那衝破牢籠的靈魂在飛翔。

　　詩作五十三〈脊樑〉是對英雄的讚頌，是對懦夫的諷刺。

　　該詩集最後一首詩作是〈從砂石場邊走過〉。這是詩人許其正先生和他的靈魂一起哭著喊著要回歸自然的吶喊；對此，我們似乎無話可說，只能表示贊同，並為我們在拯救這顆星球的生態平衡方面所表現出的怠慢感到自責。許其正先生，我敬重並熱烈地擁抱你，因為你是一位真正的詩人。這部詩集裡所收錄的詩作大都是上乘之作，不少篇目在此之前我已經讀過。太棒了！許先生，我的好朋友！

（楊宗澤　譯）

2007 年 2 月 1 日　世界詩人季刊

　　按：本文作者為英國國際名詩人，現居利物浦。

Dr. Hsu Chisheng:"REAPPEARANCE"

Zacharoula   Gaitanaki

Poems   (Chinese - English), Translated by YANG
ZONGZE Cover designer: Mr. Diablo, Editor - in - chief:
Dr. Zhang Zhi Pages: 158, ISBN: 978-09637599-6-5, 1000
copies,   Price: 15 eur

> *Waiting patiently*
> *winter will pass away*
> *Spring will come soon*
> *warmth   will   come*
> *accompanying it. (page 19)*

Dr. Hsu Chicheng's new collection of poetry entitled
"REAPPEARANCE" is an excellent book with fine verses
(51 pieces).

I enjoyed his poetry, especially his poems: "The view

in a Winter Morning" (page 21), "Light the Lamp" (p. 23), "Steel - like" (p. 31), "Taipei Always is the Starting Point of revival" (p. 53-55), "Search for mails" (p. 63), "Ah, Firefly……" (p. 79), "Doing my Best" (p. 81-83) and "Mr. Huang's Orchard" (p. 129 - 131).

From the Winter to Spring, Dr. Hsu, with his book, give us an "OMEN" (p. 65) and two most important questions:

"Do you feel joyful inwardly?
Do you smile to yourself?"

The answer is: be happy and "FOLLOW YOUR OWN WAY" (p. 45):

"You may wear Western style clothes
You may eat Japanese food
You may drive imported limousine
You may speak English
You may enjoy foreign films
Even you may dye your hair as a foreign people...

But, bear in mind: Your heart must be your own
You must always follow your own way!".

Retirement isn't the end of life. It's the starting point for creation and a new route, a new trip. We are thankful to poetry because it cures and it's a real friend. The poet writes "FOR HER" (p. 139):

"It is she, it is just she
   Who has such a wonderful charm
   That attracts me that deeply
   Perhaps it is doomed
   That I will fall for her
   Without any consideration of fame
   Since I meet her
   For her, I am even
   Lost in thought day and night.
   For her, I am pining but never give up
   She is just
   —Poetry. "

Poetry is "A hope in Winter", a sunbeam "in a Winter

morning", a bud and a seed. It's a firefly, "a little star", "*a dream / colorful and full of spirituality*"... Poetry is a gift and Dr. Hsu is a very lucky man because he has a special talent: he is an authentic poet...

Special thanks to Dr. Yang Zongze, the famous contemporary Chinese poet and translator. With his job, we read in English the poems of Dr. Hsu Chicheng and we enjoy his beautifully written.

評介《重現》

札查露拉‧格坦娜契

　　許其正著作：中英對照詩集《重現》，英譯：楊宗澤，封面設計：張智，主編：張智，158 頁，國際統一書號：978-09637599-6-5，初版印數 1000 冊，定價：15 歐元。

　　且耐心等等

冬天走了
春天很快會來
溫暖會
跟著到來（第 19 頁）

　　許其正博士新出版書名為「重現」的詩集是一本含括 51 首好詩的優良書籍。

　　我欣賞他的詩，尤其《冬晨即景》（第 21 頁）、《點亮燈盞》（第 23 頁）、《如鋼似鐵》（第 31 頁）、《甦醒總從台北起腳》（第 53—55 頁）、《探取信件》（第 63 頁）、《螢火蟲呀，你……》（第 79 頁）、《傾盡全身心力》（第 81—83 頁）和《黃家果園》（第 129—131 頁）。

　　從冬天到春天，許博士給予我們一個好《兆》（第 65 頁）和兩個最重要的問題：

　　你，心懷竊喜嗎？
　　你，笑容暗藏嗎？

　　答案是：要快樂並且《做自己》（第 45 頁）：

　　衣服可以穿西裝結領帶
　　吃食可以是日本料理

代步的可以是克來斯勒
講的可以是滿口英語
看的可以是洋片
甚至跟著流行染髮……

但是心一定要是自己的
——我要做我自己！

　　退休不是人生的終點。它是創作和人生新路、新旅
程的起點。我們感謝詩，因為它可治癒疾患，乃吾人的
好友。詩人在《為了她》（第139頁）中寫著：

就是她，就是她
具有這麼大的魅力
緊緊地吸引住了我
不知是否前生註定
從第一次遇見她
我便不計毀譽代價
一頭栽了進去
為了她，我甚至
日思夜想，癡迷不悟
為她醉得人消瘦，死生不渝

就是她，就是她
——詩

詩是「冬天裡的希冀」，「冬晨」的微曦，一枚新芽和一顆種子。它是一隻螢火蟲，「一顆小星星，」「*一個夢/多彩而靈動的*」……詩是一樣禮物，而許博士是幸運的，因為他是一個專擅的天才：他是一位名副其實的詩人……。

特別感謝中國現代名詩人和翻譯家楊宗澤。由於他的努力，我們能拜讀許博士的英譯詩，並欣賞他的完美創作。

（雅靜譯）

2008.7.11 亞特蘭大新聞「亞城園地」文學週刊
2008.7.15 青溪論壇
2008.8.08 世界詩人（中英對照）
2008.8.21 菲律賓世界日報文藝副刊

當詩花翩然而至

——讀許其正博士新著中英雙語詩集《重現》

西安　王式儉

　　沉潛和蘊釀乃屬必然
　　當時候來臨，春天回返
　　我就化蝶，翩然
　　飛成一朵閃亮的詩花
　　　　　　——許其正〈化蝶〉

　　正當中斷九年之后，兩會復談，兩岸週末包機、大陸赴台旅遊簽署協議，即將實施之際，收到彼岸詩友許其正先生惠贈的新著詩集《重現》，心裡感到格外欣慰。許先生從教 33 年，1998 年退休后，在詩壇戮力耕耘，忍受孤獨和寂寞，潛心從事自己心愛的閱讀和寫作，近年來，詩花飛揚，碩果累累。先後出版《海峽兩岸遊蹤》、《胎記》、《心的翅膀》等多部詩集，其中，《海峽兩岸遊蹤》出版中英、中希對照兩種，《胎記》出版中英、中蒙、中希對照三種，《心的翅膀》出版希、英、法、意、中對照一種。這部新近由環球文化出版社出版的中英對照詩集《重現》收詩 51 首，是作者 2007 年發表百餘首詩作的選集。作者在序言中說："前年下半年起，我開始在網路上看報紙，其中一項很重要的目的是，另外找一塊在國外可以發表作品戮力耕耘的園地。天從我願，我終於找到了。那就是美國亞特蘭大新聞的文學副刊《亞城園地》週刊。我於去年 1 月 16 日電郵送出第一首詩〈爬山感懷〉，三天後，即 1 月 19 日竟奇跡似地刊出了。真快！欣喜之餘，我陸續送出拙詩，一週 1 到 7 首。一年下來，我在該刊發表了 107 首。這些詩，我原計畫以《亞城一年》為書名出版，卻因中英對照印起來太厚太多，而且有些龐雜，我剔除了一部分，因沒有全數收入，所以改以《重現》書名出版"。

　　中國詩歌歷來有述志為本，順美匡惡的傳統，這部詩集引人注目的仍是那些關注社會民生的詩，如：〈走春一說〉、〈蘇醒總從台北起腳〉、〈探取信件〉、〈拯救屈原〉、〈爽鳩呀〉、〈找金伯伯去〉等，這些詩，不僅立意深遠，藝術手法也相當純熟。詩人在〈走春一說〉中譴責了那些把春天的好處"整碗捧去"的"走春的政客"；〈蘇醒總從台北起腳〉採用象徵性語言，告訴那些空口哺舌者，如不吸取教訓，"再厚的防火牆都會被燒毀。"詩中寫道：那些被空口哺舌們口水噴得／呼呼大睡的冬眠之動植物們／這時便漸漸甦醒過來了／／很奇怪，每次都一樣／蘇醒總從台北起腳／那只是星星之火／卻能向四處蔓延／。這兩首詩均採用示現和戲劇性自對方式，讀后讓人感到耳目一新。〈探取信件〉採用象徵手法，暗示了詩人祈盼兩岸和解、世界和平的急切心情。詩中這樣寫道：口銜橄欖枝的鴿子呀／你在哪裡？／願你在日落之前／盡快帶來和平！〈拯救屈原〉表達了詩人對詩歌現狀的不滿和戮力拯救詩歌的決心，詩中他這樣寫道：時至今日／詩也受盡委屈／划龍船多有詩意卻於事無補／屈原已成曠世冤魂／詩也已經只有小眾參與／更要我們戮力拯救／不能讓它也與屈原同沉江底／／讓忠義和詩花隨時隨處綻放／千秋萬世，香火永續傳承。〈爽鳩呀〉表達了時代對維持社會安定、公正和平的殷切期待。爽鳩，鷹也，故為司寇，主盜賊，系古官名。春秋時，即有司寇之官，清時稱刑部尚書為大司寇。〈找金伯伯去〉表達了詩人對社會道德和良知的呼喚。一個人一生做一件好事並不難，難的是一生做好事。詩中金伯伯是學校的一名工友，他的離去為什麼讓全校師生感到悲傷和失落？原來他在世的時候，學校各個角落，事無巨細，從門窗玻璃到桌椅板凳，無論哪裡有困難，只要找金伯伯，都能得到滿意的解決，同學們在金伯伯那裡感受到無微不至的關愛。中國古代哲學家老子曾說"大音希聲，大巧若拙。"讀許其正先生的詩時常讓我感覺到老子所說的"大巧若拙"的智慧。他的詩，初讀似乎讓人感覺平平常常，並無什麼新奇的字眼，但兩三遍后，卻讓人感到餘味無窮。這部詩集中一些寫人生感悟的詩。如〈爬山感懷〉、〈大板根〉、〈一雙皮鞋〉、〈白目佛〉等也很耐讀。此外，一些寫自然景觀的詩，如〈翔飛的蒲公英〉、〈風碎步而行〉、〈歡笑的荷田〉、〈難得的夏午〉 等也都寫得純美和飄逸，給我留下深刻的印象。

　　唐代散文家韓愈有一篇雜文〈龍說〉稱："龍噓氣成雲，龍乘是氣，可徜徉窮乎雲間，其所憑依乃其所自為也。"文章取類至深，寄託甚廣。許先生老有所為，退休后適時找到屬於自己的人生平台，開創出人生的第二個春天。近年來或得於山水之助，或出於山水之外，山水自然、國事家事無不歷覽，既覽必發為詩，並且其詩益工，其志意愈高，正如昌黎所言：其所憑依乃其所自為也。

2008 年 7 月 18 日亞特蘭大新聞《亞城園地》
2008 年 7 月 19 日菲律賓世界日報文藝副刊

賞閱許其正新詩集「重現」

湯為伯

　　我在文藝田畦裡墾耕了近半個世紀，文藝成果雖然算不上大豐收，倒還差強人意；但最使我感到得意的事，是在此近五十年筆耕歲月裡，結識了數愈上百的文耕同好。播種小說的，播種散文的，撒播新詩的，專耕文藝理論的，或耕戲劇的……。儘管各自耕種的類別有異，但都在文藝大範圍內，且都是用腦、用筆、用稿紙（現在有用電腦的）及時光等珍貴的種籽來播撒，隨後萌芽，茁壯，開花，然後結成人類所需要的精神果實，營養著兆億人的心靈，所以說筆耕者都是人類心靈的營養師。

　　我與上百位相識的筆耕同好中，經常保持連絡的大約有三分之一，保持最緊密連繫者僅十幾位，默默而勤奮筆耕新詩的多年好友許其正就是這十幾位筆耕文友之一。

　　許其正之所以與我友誼不渝，是基於數種原因：一是因為我昔日服務軍職期間，大多駐防高、屏地區，所以我的文章也大多投寄在南部幾家報紙及雜誌上，而許其正是屏東潮州人，他是中學教師，曾為五專講師，也曾被鳳山陸軍官校以副教授之名聘為該校社團文藝創作指導教師，他的詩或散文也大多在南部各文藝刊物上發表，因而彼此的姓名經常在各刊物上相遇，隨後我們都參與中國文藝協會南部分會，在每月舉行一次座談會中常常晤面，由相遇進而相知。那時高雄市新聞處經常不定期舉辦南部（高、屏、南）文藝作家全島風景名勝旅遊與參觀全島重大建設，因此與許其正接觸更頻些，彼此瞭解也更多些。他的個性溫和內向，不愛出風頭，和我性情類似。

　　二是由於我的另一半娘家是潮州鎮近鄰的新埤鄉 X 農村。許其正當時在新埤國中任教兼教務主任，也有親戚在該村，對該村很熟悉，因此他對我這個屏東女婿產生幾分親切感，當然我也以半個屏東人的身分與他攀上親戚的關係。

　　三是因為我與許其正年齡較為接近。他只比我小八歲，年紀相近，彼此的觀念鴻溝也就不會太寬。

　　許其正於 1960 年開始筆耕文藝，以詩作為主，散文次之，兼及小說和戲劇。他已出版詩集十冊，散文六冊，都是在各刊物發表的作品中精選彙集成冊的。其中並有中英對照、中希對照、中蒙對照。國際詩歌翻譯研究中心及國際藝術文化學院並各頒發給他榮譽文學博士學位。此種殊榮實在得之不易。

　　許其正的詩作特色是詩境深邃，而文字表達明朗，使人易讀易解，不像目前許多新詩，是在耍文字遊戲，詩句與題目似乎毫無關係，讓人讀之再三，像是瀏覽印象派西洋畫般的，只見那是色彩繽紛一塊畫布，欲知內容必須請教畫家本人。

　　當然賞詩者也好，賞畫者也好，各有不同的愛好，如同飲食者一樣，有愛辣味，有愛甜味，有愛苦酸味，但正常口味應是不太鹹，不太甜，不太酸辣，如此對身體健康才有裨益。許其正的詩就是這種正味而清淡的口味。

　　由於許其正的詩風明朗易懂，所以他的詩頗多被譯成外文。

　　許其正的詩和散文，我賞閱過無數，過往者在此不提，在此僅將他於 2008 年 5 月，由重慶環球文化出版社出版的詩集「重現」中英對照裡 51 首詩作中，隨意舉例其中三首，以供讀友觀其概要。例如 ──

冬晨即景

偶然抬頭，在這冬日清晨
但見好些一夜未眠的晨星
各自瑟縮天邊一角
已露疲態，漸見暗淡

不該下班了嗎？
卻仍一步一回首
不知還留戀什麼？
唉，還留戀什麼？

天可憐見，太陽
已擁著強光奔來
勢如長江裡的後浪
匆匆，急於大展才華......

　　這首詩把大自然景致賦予人格化，生命化。作者對星星說話，同時也等於代表讀者對星星說話，也描繪出冬天早晨晴朗的天空美景。此詩成年人可以賞讀，幼童也愛閱讀。

　　例如 ——

為了她

就是她，就是她
具有這麼大的魅力
緊緊地吸引住了我
不知是否前生註定
從第一次遇見她
我便不計毀譽代價
一頭栽了進去
為了她，我甚至
日思夜想，癡迷不悟
為她醉得人消瘦，死生不渝
就是她，就是她
——詩

　　許其正對詩的癡迷，對詩的深愛，他自己形容成是他初戀的情人，相信他的愛妻讀了這首詩也許會吃醋，卻又感動不已。他自 21 歲便開始與詩相愛，如今他已七十高齡，與詩相愛已半個世紀，算是金婚紀念的喜年了！50 年來，他不但對詩堅貞不渝，同時詩的果實也很豐碩累累。

　　例如 ——

做自己

衣服可以穿西裝結領帶
吃食的可以是日本料理
代步的可以是克萊斯勒
講的可以是滿口英語
看的可以是洋片
甚至可以跟著流行染髮……
但是心一定要是自己的
── 要做我自己！

　　這首詩是警示年輕人，不要崇洋過了頭，愛時尚是
無可厚非，但不要忘了自己根本，祖宗忘了，國家也忘
了，心甘情願要做外國人，那是最可恥的事。無獨立人
格，無主宰自己思想能力者，是軟弱無能的人。

　　我枚舉上列三題，並非代表這三首是「重現」詩集
中最傑出的詩作，而是這三首詩有描景的，有抒情的，
有寫意的等類別差異，其實書內多首妙詩佳作，我不忍
心驚擾她，留待愛詩的讀友自己去細心賞讀吧！

　　「重現」詩集能在重慶環球文化出版社出版，是件
大幸事，因為該出版社所出版之文學書籍，不僅經銷全

中國，並且贈送全世界各國大圖書館，以及各國的所有
大學圖書館，讓眾多愛好文學的知識人士皆能閱讀其詩
作，是非常難得之事，怎能不算是大幸事？每位文學家
或其他類別的著作家，不都期望自己的作品有愈多的閱
讀者愈好嗎？

　　該出版社所出版之文學書籍，大多事先由該社專任
外文翻譯員譯成 ── 或英文，或德文，或法文或其他國
家文字，即以中外文對照方式出版。許其正的詩大多由
該社譯成外文 ── 英文、日文、希臘文等等出版，以行
銷國外，因此他的文學名聲，在外國比在國內響亮得
多。值得羨佩，值得慶賀。

　　　2008.8 修正定稿
　　　2008.8.8 亞特蘭大新聞「亞城園地」文學週刊

　　按：本文作者，江西九江人，寫作以散文、小品為主，兼及
　　　　新詩、評論。

BOOK REVIEW:《REAPPEARANCE》

Dr. R.K.SINGH

Hsu Chicheng. ***REAPPEARANCE***. (Chinese-English). Trans. Yang Zongze. Publishers: The Earth Culture Press (USA). Chongqing City, P.R.China, 2008, pp. 153. Price: US$ 15.00. ISBN 978-0-9637599-6-5/A.061

Getting old is not only natural but also a blessing from God. It is an opportunity to rejuvenate oneself by re-living with hope in life. Hsu Chicheng, a renowned contemporary Chinese poet, writer and translator, with an oeuvre of 15 books, including eight poetry collections, stands for aging gracefully. A specialist in reading and writing, and widely translated in Greek, Japanese, English and Mongolian, Hsu looks at the aged and aging respectfully.

There are people over 50 who feel more like 35, or

even less. Hsu Chicheng, at 70, confidently looks for "another world" and "another spring" as "a just born". "I am only a baby," says the retired academic.　He feels free: "I have got rid of the fetters of time and watch."

I find the poet inspiring as he is not discouraged by the age he has reached. Rather, poetry makes him young; he tries to do or get better by not stopping his creative faculty from thinking and dreaming just as he keeps "climbing a mountain" or "having a stroll in spring" or "waiting patiently" or "remasticating again and again".

The bilingual poet and special editor-in-chief of *The World Poets Quarterly* , Hsu Chicheng makes aging an enriching experience. As a poet of hope, he observes life *a la* natural cycle and rhythm:

> "Is it time for you to get off work?
> Yet you look back again and again
> What and whom are you reluctant to part with?
> ….
> Look! The sun
> Is coming with its strong rays
> Like the surging waves

In Yangtze River..."

> *('The View in a Winter Morning')*

and

"The collapse of winter, a tyrant
To welcome spring's arrival
That day
The world will be fully filled with
Sunlight, flowers and joy"

> *('A Hope in Winter')*

and

"Yes, she is busy indeed

…

Yet she doesn't feel tired and works day and night
Always appearing joyful, beaming with smile
Her best wish is to see
All things on earth come back to life
The growing, blossoming..."

> *('Spring is Busy Now')*

The poet seeks to live afresh, making sense of the

contemporary life, naturally, joyously, and talking, singing, running or walking fast like a Youngman, or even dancing like a drunk person.　His poems, as Hsu acknowledges in the preface to *Reappearance*, bespeak a return to youth and childhood:

> "We raise our heads and overlook, expecting another world
> We raise our heads and overlook, expecting another spring."
>
> *('Reappearance')*

He turns spiritual as he declares:

> "When spring comes and the chance appears,
> I will turn into a butterfly, flying gracefully
> Into a bright flower of poetry."
>
> *('Turning into a Butterfly')*

Another striking aspect of Hsu Chicheng's poetry is the expression of social awareness. He is deeply rooted in his native consciousness as a Taiwanese and, despite the winds of change, he follows his own way: **"I only persist in my own ideal/ I am not a migratory bird/ I love this land"** and **"I will never give in."** He sounds tense by the pulls of political changes and the pace of communication revolution just as he seems convinced that the reality is not what is real.

As he confronts the new realities facing Taiwan, Hsu Chicheng expresses his anger: **"Those politicians.../ Have taken away/ All the benefit of spring/People have to sink into the abyss of suffering."** With the disposition of a fighter, Hsu wraps his social concerns in nature imagery and makes poetry a means of protest against the nightmarish existence, sustained by swindlers, plunderers, criminals, murderers, corrupt officials and schismatic politicians et al. He ironically asks: **"How could it be like this?"** Yet, he is confident: **"Taipei always is the starting point of revival"** and **"Happiness and richness will surge."**

It seems the pressure of globalization and socioeconomic changes vis-à-vis the political identity of the Taiwanese litterateurs made Yang Zongze choose Hsu

Chicheng's poems for rendering into English.　Hsu
deserves to be more widely known and poet-translator
Yang Zongze appears textually quite subtle and effective in
communicating the Taiwanese poet's world-view, which is
rich in images of nature and society and seeks to uphold
humanity and justice. Kudos to Yang's stirring and
empathetic labour of love!

評《重現》

Dr. R.K.Singh 作

雅　靜　譯

　　《重現》（中英對照），許其正著，楊宗
澤譯，中國重慶環球文化出版社 2008 年出
版，153 頁，定價美金 15 元，國際統一編號：
isnb978-0-9637599-6-5/A061

　　變老不僅是自然現象，也是神的恩寵。它是對生命
充滿希望而重生的返老還童機會。許其正，一個當代著

名中國詩人、作家和翻譯家，以其出版 15 本著作，包括 8 本詩集，突顯其老年的優雅姿態。以一個專事閱讀和寫作者，作品被廣泛翻譯為希臘文、日文、英文和蒙古文，許無視老年屆臨，成為一個被尊崇的老年人。

有人年過 50 歲卻仍像 35 歲甚至更年輕。許其正，已經 70 歲，卻很有自信地望向"另一個天地"和"另一個春天"，如"一個剛出生的嬰兒"。"我才是一個嬰兒，"這個退休的學者這麼說。他自覺"被釋放了"："我從時間和鐘錶的枷鎖解脫出來了"。

我發現這個詩人激昂得不怕他已臻於老境。更確切地說，詩使他年輕；他試圖以思想和夢想使他的創作更上層樓，一如他"爬山"或"走春"或"耐心等等"或"反芻呀反芻"。

作為一個雙語詩人和《世界詩人季刊》的特約總編，許其正將老年視為在增進經驗。作為一個詩人，他視生命為一個自然循環和節奏：

"不該下班了嗎？
卻仍一步一回首
不知還留戀什麼？
……

天可憐見，太陽
已擁著強光奔來
勢如長江裡的後浪
匆匆，急於大展才華……"

　　　　　（冬晨即景）

而

"等待冬天這暴君崩解
等待必定到來的
那一天
讓陽光、花果和快樂
充滿人間"

　　　　　（冬天裡的希冀）

而

"是的，她忙碌著
……
可是她毫不倦怠，整日連夜
笑逐顏開，歡天喜地
她最大的希望是
世上萬物都甦醒過來，活動起來
並且繁榮起來，繽紛起來……"

（春天忙碌著）

　　詩人尋求活得鮮活，感知當代生活，灑脫自在，欣喜逾恆，高談，歡唱，年輕人般跑跳，或甚至陶醉的舞者般狂舞。他的詩，正如許在《重現》序中自認的，回到年輕和孩提時代：

　　　"我們引頸而望，但願望出一個天地來
　　　我們引頸而望，但願望出一個春天來"
　　　　　　　　　　　　　　（重現）

他鄭重地宣佈：

　　　"當時候來臨，春天回返
　　　　　我就化蝶，翩然
　　　飛成一朵閃亮的詩花"
　　　　　　　　　　（化蝶）

　　許其正另一個引人注目的面向是對社會知覺的表達。他根植於台灣本土意識，不為世風所動搖，他走他自己的路："我有我的堅持／我不是那些候鳥／我愛這塊土地"而"我絕不讓步！"他為政治的改變和交流溝通的革命而發聲，正如他相信真理不是外表顯現的真實相。

　　面對新的台灣表面相，許其正發出他的憤怒："那些政客……/ 把春天的好處/ "整碗捧去了/人民不沉溺在痛苦的深淵能奈何？"以一個戰士的情性，許以自然的意象，披著他的社會關懷，寫出向夢魘、慣性騙徒、劫掠者、罪犯、謀殺兇手、貪腐官員和分裂政客等抗議的詩。他反諷地問："怎麼會這樣？"然後他自信滿滿地說："甦醒總從臺北起腳"而"那康樂富裕就要湧現。"

　　似乎全球化和社會經濟的改變對台灣文學的壓力促使楊宗澤選擇將許其正的詩翻譯為英文的。許應更為人所知，譯者楊宗澤顯示其文本的極度精到和有效傳達台灣詩人的世界觀，富裕了自然和社會的想像，並提升了人性和正義。楊的辛勞和努力值得讚賞。

2008.8.29 亞特蘭大新聞「亞城園地」文學
週刊（雅靜譯，中英對照）
2008.11.8 世界詩人（瘦路譯，中英對照）
2008.11 India Book Chronicle（英文）
2008.11.11 菲律賓世界日報文藝副刊
2009.5.4 藝文論壇
2012.11 Breakthrough

按：本文作者為印度礦業大學教授兼人文社會科學學系主任，國際名詩人，兼及評論，已退休。

另一個春天的詩情

——讀臺灣著名詩人許其正中英文對照詩集《重現》

唐　詩

"我們在意的是下一次的約定／我們引頸而望，但願望出另一個天地來／我們引頸而望，但願望出另一個春天來"。——《重現》

這是一種充滿濃濃詩情的美好約定，也是一個佈滿悠悠畫意的良好願望。為了這個約定和願望，一個人可以在冬天裏翹首春天，在苦難中渴望幸福，在失敗中尋找成功·······

許其正先生 1939 年出生在臺灣屏東縣，今年已是古稀之年。1998 年，不滿六十歲的詩人在臺灣退休後，詩興大發，詩情不斷，寫詩不斷，一口氣出版了近十部詩集，其中僅 2007 年就在美國亞特蘭大的《亞城園地》週刊上發表 107 首詩，從其中精選 51 首成中英對照的詩集《重現》，從這一點可以看出許先生詩情的爆發力是何等的猛烈。

我審視古今中外詩壇，老年能有如此詩情的詩人不多。在國外詩人中，有創作貫穿了整個人生的歌德等大詩人，在國內的新詩人中，有老年重返詩壇創作出"歸來的歌"的艾青等大詩人，在當代大陸重慶，有著名老詩人華萬里，他老年創作的詩歌十分前衛、現代，富於探索性，被譽為中國當代豔體詩之王，新鴛鴦蝴蝶派詩人，在當代臺灣，有著名老詩人許其正，詩人到了老年靈感與詩意、詩情奔騰而來，詩如泉湧，佳構不斷，佳作迭出，形成了當代詩壇老年詩人少有的"井噴"奇觀，被譽為迎來了另一個詩的春天的詩人。

"蟄伏了十幾年／醞釀了十幾年／經過無數孤獨和寂寞的錘煉／我已準備好了／我要放開心胸，大聲鳴叫／／我要傾盡全身心力，大鳴大放／噴發出所有精心釀製的精華／噴發出所有的心血結晶／聲音鋪天蓋地，無處不在／勢如驚雷，如火山爆發，如暴風雨／所有阻滯也要棄械投降"。 ——《傾盡全身心力》

這可以說是詩人到了老年猶有滾滾詩情、滔滔靈感的真實寫照。

　　有才華的詩人是一切都可以入詩，一切皆有詩意。樸實而詩意的歌唱鄉村、田園和大自然是許先生詩歌的突出特點。在他的筆下蒲公英在神采飛揚的展現青春年華，落葉在暢談甚至呻吟，彗星不是在預言災難而是在除舊佈新，向日葵總是在迎向光明，風在田野碎步而行，春天在忙碌著並擁有巨大的魔力……一切自然的動物、植物乃至細小的微生物都會觸動詩人敏感而多情的心靈，這一切在詩人的心靈世界得到了自然而具有詩意的融合。

　　"當他寫詩的時候／不管所寫的物件是什麼／……都會有和人一樣的語言和動作／甚至心靈、精神和思想／……也都具有了生命／會活蹦亂跳，活靈活現……它們一個個都進入了他的內裏／和他融而為一了"。——《融》

　　十分明瞭而清晰的告訴讀者，大千世界的一切都可以在許先生年老而又年輕的詩性世界融合成天下美妙而哀怨，自然而厚重，樸實而深刻的詩篇……讓我們不得不佩服許先生超人的才情和過人的深思。

　　人生是許先生詩筆下吟詠的主旋律，也是他最打動人的詩篇。在這本詩集裏，詩人既有老年爬山的感懷，又有在冬天耐心等待的忍勁，希望沒有一絲憂傷的新年祈願，還有興外境的白目佛，在記憶中一再追憶的金伯伯等等……更有"但是心一定要是自己的／──我要做我自己"的直抒胸臆。

　　好的詩篇不是寫出來的，而是心靈的自然流露。詩人的《一雙皮鞋》讀來讓人的心不能不為之顫動，尤其是詩的結尾覺得詩人好像有神靈附體似的寫出了神來之筆："最高明的製鞋專家又是誰／我坦然的告訴他們：／／那最好的皮是踢到石頭會流血的真皮／我是從有生命時就開始穿了／最高明的製鞋專家則是／賜給我生命的母親"。讀著這樣的詩句，我們既嘆服詩人的機智和巧妙，又佩服詩人的深情和奇思。

　　《擺脫鎖鏈》則十分鮮明而深刻的表達了詩人那種渴望擺脫人生一切束縛和囚禁的強烈願望，但是詩人卻是從他退休後不戴手錶，這一日常生活細節中引申出了無限美好而又無限深刻的詩意："手腕上那道白白的痕跡是一道逮捕令／我那時沒有自由／我那時被鎖鏈緊緊地鎖住／／現在，我像一個囚徒，被釋放了／是自從退休以後／我可以睡到自然醒／……我是一匹無韁的野馬／愛怎樣就怎樣，要去哪里就去哪裏"。靈巧的表達了上班時的不自由和退休以後的無拘無束，讀來又自然又充滿詩意，這樣一個生活細節，被詩人心靈的陽光照耀得熠熠生輝。

　　能夠認識自己所喜愛藝術的局限或不足，只有清醒者才能做到。對詩歌現狀的揪心是許先生超出一般詩人的地方。當今詩壇外面十分冷漠，不僅大陸如此，臺灣也如此。詩歌已經微弱到可以忽略的地步了。許先生十分清醒的看到了現代詩所面臨的處境。

　　"詩也已經只有小眾參與"，因此詩人為了詩歌："日思夜想，癡迷不悟"，儘管詩人"雜處在人世間／被俗世雜務糾纏著／整日連夜奔忙／卻不能找不到定居的地方"。為此，詩人在《垂釣什麼》一詩中寫道："除了靈感，還有詩意"。

　　讓我頗有同感的是《拯救屈原》一詩所爆發出的對當前詩歌的憂心如焚："龍船向前，向前再向前／大家戮力划著／我們不是在玩遊戲／是為了拯救屈原／是為了拯救詩／／……屈原已成曠古冤魂／詩也已經只有小眾參與／更要我們戮力拯救／不能讓它也與屈原同沉江底"。

　　是啊，當今詩壇，不論中國還是世界其他國家，詩歌仿佛由過去在藝術高高的山巔沉降到了生活的江底，沉降到了藝術的江底，沉降到了人們娛樂和心靈的江底……儘管事實上詩歌從來就是孤獨而寂寞的"精英藝術"。

　　面對此種情況，許先生向所有的詩人發出了號召："不怕千辛萬苦，汗流浹背／我們要拯救屈原／也要不停地拯救詩／讓忠義和詩花隨時隨處綻放／千秋萬世，香火永續傳承……"這種大義凜然，氣勢磅礴的吶喊，已經足以深深地打動每一位詩人，難道詩人們還不戮力划著詩歌的龍船衝向這個熱情不斷產生也不斷消失的喧囂世界？

　　與時代結合的詩篇是最有生命力的詩篇，是大詩人的標誌。渴望和平，痛批當局是許先生詩歌的又一突出特點。詩人在《探取信件》裏寫道："每天我都向信箱探取信件／不管信件有多少都令我失望／我等的信件怎麼都沒來？"是什麼樣的信件讓我們的老詩人如此盼望？尤其是"日子不停地過去／不僅我的額頭疊出了許多山川／連頭上也堆滿了厚厚的雪／日暮黃昏越逼越近／我越來越感到等不及了／憂心如焚，燒灼我心"，我們的心也與老詩人的焦慮一起陡然增加，我們在剎那間也仿佛憂心如焚了。"口銜橄欖枝的鴿子呀／你在哪里？願你在日落之前／儘快帶來和平"。"日落"在此可作多種解釋，既可以是自然界的日落，也可以是人生的日落……無論作何種解釋，都是詩人所不願意看見的結果，日落越逼近越體現詩人渴盼和平早來的焦急。

　　在《新年祈願》裏再次寫到："但願新的一年／日日是好日／日日都是彩色的／舞動著快樂與和平／沒有一絲憂傷不快／人間的不幸從此不再"。原來，我們尊敬的老詩人不僅要為拯救詩歌奮力地划船，而且在面對這個戰爭和自然災害不斷的世界，是那麼強烈的呼喚和平，這樣的詩篇無疑是偉大的詩篇，哪里是什麼個人小圈子的無病呻吟？這樣的詩篇無疑應該受到包括詩人們在內的所有世人的高度讚賞！

　　能否直面當世，既是詩人勇氣的體現，也是詩人人格的高度彰顯。詩人對臺灣當局的鞭撻和批判也是非常到位，讀來讓人既佩服他的勇氣，又嘆服他的率真。在《走春一說》詩中，詩人這樣寫到："怎麼這麼奇怪？／今年全球普遍暖冬……世界各地景氣隨氣溫同步回升／唯獨臺灣不明顯？／仍寒風刺骨，令人驚顫／到處見失業、不快樂、自殺？……／／不為別的／因為那些走春的政客／把春天的好處／整碗捧去了／人民不沉溺在痛苦的深淵能奈何？"讀到此處，我突然覺得，我們先前可愛、可敬、可親的許先生，是那樣毫不留情地橫眉怒視著那些給人民帶來痛苦的臺灣的政客們。

　　優秀的詩人總會著力經營自己的特色並充分展示自己的特色。許先生的詩不僅充盈著對自然、田園、山水等的奇思妙想，而且更有對人生風雲變幻的詩意展示，還有對當局無情的批判和嘲弄。面對這個風雨不斷的社會，在《大板根》一詩裏，詩人借一棵樹這樣表白道：＂堅持不離開這塊土地／不管干擾的外力如何：／風雨再大，霜雪再冷，炙陽再烈／都動搖不了我這個信念／我一定要在這裏堅強挺立／堅強挺立，直到永遠⋯⋯＂

　　詩人的高貴和詩篇的珍貴不是由詩人自己評定。不用作更多的評述，許先生的詩歌創作獲得的那些世界性的詩歌獎項是當之無愧的。有光芒的老詩人，讓我們年輕詩人感到汗顏，值得敬畏。

　　我們在意的是詩人下一次詩意的約定，我們引頸而望，但願望出詩人另一個詩歌的春天來，我們引頸而望，但願望出詩人另一個春天的詩情來。

2009.3.23 於重慶核桃村

　　　作者簡介：唐詩，本名唐德榮，出生於重慶市榮昌縣，管理學博士，榮譽文學博士，中國作家協會會員、國際漢語詩歌協會常務理事、中外散文詩歌學會主席團委員、國際詩歌翻譯研究中心榮譽主席。出版詩文集《走向那棵樹》、《花朵還未走到秋天》、《走遍靈魂的千山萬嶺》、《螞蟻之光》（中英對照）、《花朵與回聲》、《為每個人服好務》、《把村莊搬到紙上》、《穿越時間的紙張》等多部。詩作翻譯成十餘種文字，入選大學教材。中國作家協會《詩刊》社、重慶市文聯、中國詩學中心曾聯合舉辦唐詩詩歌作品研討會。參加23屆青春詩會。獲重慶市文學獎，臺灣薛林懷鄉青年詩獎，中國作家協會《詩刊》社藝術文庫優秀詩集獎，希臘國際文學藝術獎，國際最佳詩人獎等多項獎勵。

Poetics of another Spring

Tang　Shi

—— Reading " Reappearance" (Chinese- English) by Hsu ChiCheng,a famous poet from Taiwan

"What we mind most is the next time/ We raise our heads and overlook , expecting another world/ We raise our heads and overlook, expecting another spring". (Reappearance)

This is a beautiful appointment filled with poetics,

and a willful wish which is picturesque. For this appointment and wish, a person may look forward spring in winter, may long for happiness in tribulation, and may search for success in failure...

In 1939, Mr. Hsu was born in Pingtung County of Tiawan, and he is now in his seventies. In 1998 when he retired at the left side of 60 in Taiwan, the poet is full of poetic inspiration, and he has published nearly ten collections of poetry in a breath. In 2007, he published 107 poems on a weekly poetry magazine in Atlanta of the USA., from which his 51 choice poems are collected into a collection entitled *Reappearance* (Chinese-English). From this we can see how vigorous is Mr.Hsu creativity.

Examining domestic and oversea poetry forum, we seldom see an old poet with such passionate poetic. Overseas, Goethe's writing runs throughout his life; domestically, Ai Qing returns to the forum of poetry in his old age, to compose "songs of return", and in contemporary Chongqing, Hua Wanli is a senior poet who's poetry is modern, advance guard, full of exploration, for which he is honored as "king of amorous poems in contemporary China" and a poet of the new mandarin ducks and butterflies school. And Hsu ChiCheng, a famous poet from contemporary Taiwan, is prolific in writing poems in his advance age. His inspiration and creation gush like a fountain of spring, which forms a marveious spectacle of "blowout", and Hsu is hence a poet who embraces a new spring.

" *After hibernating and preparing/ For more than ten years / Through the tempering by loneliness / I am ready now/ I will do my best to shout loudly// I will do my best to shout loudly/ To spout all the essence I have made for long/ To spout all the fruit of my industriousness/ My voice will spread here and there/ Overwhelming like thunder, like volcanic eruption/ all what to block me will lay down their arms*".

— *Doing M y Best*

This can be regarded as a portrait of the poet's image in his advanced age when he is still full of inspiration and poetic feeling.

Everything can be subject matter in a poem for a gifted poet, and there is poetry at that. Mr. Hsu's poetry is characterized by his simple singing of the countryside, gardens and the great nature. Under his pen, dandelions are exhibiting their youth while flying; falling leaves are talking, even whispering; instead of predicting disasters, comets are welcoming in the new and bidding adieu to the old; sunflowers are greeting the sunshine; the wind is minicing its steps in the field; spring is busy while possessing a great witchcraft...all natural animals, plants, and even microorganism will touch the poet's amorous and sensitive heart, all of which is harmonized naturally and poetically in the poet's world of soul.

"Each of the image in his poems/ No matter it is/ Animals or plants/ Has act and words like man/ Even in soul, spirit and thought/ Mountains, rivers, and buildings/ Also have lives/ Jumping joyfully, lively like children/ This is very simple/ For he is always deeply touched by the image/ Therefore, there can enter into his inner world / One after another/ And melt into his soul".

—— *Melting*

It is quite clear to readers that everything in the boundless universe, in Mr. Hsu's world of poetry which is both old and new, can be subject matter constitute poems which are plaintive and wonderful, massive and natural, simple and profound. This wins our admiration for Mr. Hsu's rare gift and deep thought.

Human life is the theme under Mr. Hsu's pen, with which he touches readers' heart and soul. In this collection of poetry, the poet expresses his emotion of mountain climbing in an advance age, his patience of waiting in winter, his new year wishing without any trace of melancholy, the Buddha, and golden uncle in his memories...Still more, direct lyrical expression such as *"but the heart must be my own/ --I want to be myself"*.

A good poem is not made, but it is an outpouring of the heart and soul. The reader's heart throbs with the poet's *A Pair of Leather Shoes;* the end of the poem is particularly wonderfull and felicitious: *"And who is the best shoes-expert/ I tell them frankly:// The best leather is a kind of real leather that will shed blood when knocking stone/ I began to wear them since my birth/ The best shoe-expert is my mother/ who gifts me life"*. Reading such lines, we cannot but admire the poet's wit and skill, as well as his deep affection and uncommon thought.

Getting rid of fetters trenchantly and profoundly expresses the poet's strong desire to shake off all human bondage and captivity, but the poet draws poetry of boundless beauty and fathomless depth from the daily triviality of not wearing a watch after retirement: *"the white trace around the wrist is an order of arrest/ at that time I had no freedom/ I was chained fast with a chain// now, like a prisoner, I am freed/ since I am retired/ I can sleep until I awake naturally/...I am an unbridled horse/ to do anything my own way, to go anywhere I like"*. The pressure at work and the liberty after retirement are deftly expressed naturally and poetically. Such a triviality in life is illumined by sunshine in the poet's heart.

Only he who has a sober mind can realize his limitations or shortcomings in the art he enjoys. Mr. Hsu's anxiety about the status quo of poetry elevates him above the other poets. Contemporary poetry is cold-shouldered: not only in Mainland China, but also in Taiwan. Poetry only exerts a feeble influence, so much so that it can be neglected.Mr. Hsu clearly sees the status which faces modern poetry.

"*Poetry involves only a small circle of readers*". For the sake of poetry poets "*think and ponder day and night, obsessed and infatuated*"; although poets are "*mixed in the mortal world/ entangled in earthly sundries/ rushing and running around day and night/ but find no place to settle down*". Therefore, the poet produces such line in "*what to angle: except for inspiration, poetry lingers*".

What strikes a sympathetic chord in me is the poet's worries about the current poetry, which is expressed in *To Save Qu Yuan*: "*Dragon boats are marching foreward / We all try our best to paddle/ We are not playing/ But saving Qu Yuan/ And saving poetry//...Qu Yuan has been an unjust-treated soul for thousand years/ And poetry has got into a narrow lane/ Therefore, we must do our best, with one mind in a join/ To save Qu Yuan and poetry".*

Yes, poetry, from China to any country throughout the world, seems to be depositing downward to the bed of life from the high artistic peak of yore, to the river bed of art, to the river bed of people's entertainment... though actually poetry has always been "art of the elites" which is lonely and lonesome.

Facing such a situatuon, Mr. Hsu calls on all the poets: " *No fear of toils, No fear of sweating/ We must save Qu Yuan/ We must save poetry/ To let the flowers of poetry appear everywhere/ From generation to generation...".* Such a virgorous and awe-unspiring battle cry in adequate to move each and every poet. Shouldn't poets spare no efforts to row the dragon boat of poetry toward the noisy world where fervor flows and passion passes?

A poem in combination with the times is a poem of life force, and it is the symbol of a great poet. Another feature of Mr. Hsu's poetry is to yearn for peace and to criticize the authorities. In *To Probe into Letters,* the poet writes:*"I open my mailbox for mails every day/ yet it makes me disappionted each time/ For the letter I am waiting has not arrived yet?"* After all, what letter is our veternal poet waiting for? Particularly, *"As time flies away/ Wrinkle appear on my face like mountains/ And my head has been covers with snow now/ The dusk of life is closing to me / I am waiting, fidgety or restless/ As an ant in a hot pot"*. Our worries grow with the old poet and, in an instant, we seem to be burning with worries. *" O, the pegion with an olive branch in mouth/ Where are you now?/ I wish you would come together with peace / Before the sunset"*. The word "sunset" here is open in many interpretations; both natural sunset and sunset in human life…Whatever the interpretation is, the poet hales to see setting of the sun. The closer the sunset, the more anxious the poet's yearning for peace.

In *New Year Wishes*, the poet again writes: *" May in the New Year/ Each day is a luck day/ Each day is a colourful day/ Full of joy and peace / No pain or misfortune/ Will appear in the world"*. The veternal poet whom we respect does not limit himself in sparing no effects rowing his boat to save poetry, but he calls for peace in the world plagued with wars and natural disasters. Such poems merit great poems; who says they are wishy-washy things? Such poems merit high praises from people all over the world!

To face up to the present world not only shows the poet's courage, but it also displays the poet's personality. His scourge and criticism about Taiwan authorities wins people's admiration for his courage and frankness. In *Of " Having a Stroll in the country in spring"*, the poet writes: *"How strange it is?/ This year the warmer winter appears the whole globe/...Recovery appears in the whole world/ However, Taiwan is still envoloped with cold wind/ Unemploymen, disappionted ones and suicile/ can be found here and there//...Why.../Because those politicians of "Having a stroll in spring"/ Have taken away / All the benefit of spring/ People have to sink into the abyss of suffering"*. Reading such lines, I suddenly feel that Mr. Hsu, who is dear, lovable, and respectable, seems to spare no efforts in glowering at those poliicians who incur affliction upon people in Taiwan.

A distinguished poet takes care to nurture his own feature while bringing it into full play. Besides full of wonderful ideals and thinking about the nature, field, rivers and mountains, poems by Mr. Hsu poetically exhibit human winds and clouds, while ruthlessly criticizing and ridiculing the authorities. Facing the society which never lacks winds and rains, the poet, in *The Main Root,* thus professes through a tree: *" I will never leave this land/ No matter how external force interfere/ The wind, rain, snow and burning sun/ Can not shake my faith/ I will stand here erectly/ Towering uprightly eternally"*.

The poet's nobleness and the poem's treasure are not evaluated by the poet himself. No need for any further comment, Mr. Hsu is worthy of the international poetry awards he got from his poetry creation. As a veteran poet shing with rays of light, Mr. Hsu is awe-inspiring and he overshadows us young poets.

We pay close attention to the poet's next poetic appointment. And we tiptoe to look forward, in the hope of finding another poetic spring from the poet, we tiptoe to look forward, in the hope of finding another spring poetics from the poet.

2009.11.29 亞特蘭大新聞「亞城園地」文學週刊

2011.5.8 世界詩人（中英對照）

按：本文作者為大陸名詩人，評論家，現居重慶。

POETIC RYTHM AS LIFE RYTHM

Israel luiza carol

Comments about "Birthmark" by HSU Chicheng, The Earth Culture Press 2006.

What impressed me most about the poems of Hsu Chicheng was their special rhythmical quality that seemed to mirror the rhythm of life itself. I cannot comment the sound effects of the stanzas, because I can't read Chinese. But the English translations helped me get an idea about the rhythmical aspects of the poet's thoughts, of some grammar structures and some images. As a whole, I had a general feeling that poetry rhythm is used by the author as a means to integrate his own personality into the universe. Poetry rhythm may be perceived as a bridge between the inner rhythm (of heart throbs, breaths, feelings and thoughts expressed by grammar structures and words) and the rhythm of the world (of season changes in nature, age changes in human evolution, history changes in society evolution).

Let us look at the first part of the poem "A Waltz of White Clouds". Here we can find six stanzas sharing exactly the same grammatical structure, and we can follow a ternary rhythm of repetitive groups of 3 images arranged according to the following pattern: ABC (first stanza), BCD (second stanza), CDE (third stanza), DEF (fourth stanza), EFA (fifth stanza),FAB (sixth stanza). Here is the "waltz" of images that ends with the beginning, suggesting the season changes, where each end is a new beginning:

> *"A group of white pigeons*
> *has flown into cotton wadding.*
> *Has the moonlight seen it?*
> *Have you seen it?*
>
> *A group of cotton waddings*
> *has flown into the moonlight.*
> *Has the reedflowers seen it?*
> *Have you seen it?*

A group of moonlight
has flown into the reedflowers.
Has the thick fog seen it?
Have you seen it?

A group of reedflowers
has flown into the thick fog.
Have the snowflakes seen it?
Have you seen it?

A group of thick fog
has flown into snowflakes
Have the white pigeons seen it?
Have you seen it?

A group of snowflakes
has flown into the white pigeons.
Has the cotton wadding seen it?
Have you seen it?"

In the above stanzas, the last repetitive question *"Have you seen it?"* is a direct invitation for the reader to participate emotionally in this rhythmical change of shapes and colors. After the above six stanzas comes the second part of the poem, where the reader may find the same images used in a different rhythm, like in a new waltz executed by the same dancers. There is a suggestion of a "never ending" dance in this poem, as well as in many other poems.

In the poem "Reading A Letter", the feelings of the person who has written the letter are passed on to the person who reads it, through a chain of rhythmical images, as if the soul warmth were transmitted through the words. Here is the whole poem:

"I don't know
whether because there is so deep a love feeling
in this letter that I feel
as if each word in this letter is
scalding to the touch

I don't know
whether because each word in this letter
is so scalding to the touch

that I feel as if
the letter is burning

I don't know
whether because the letter is burning
that I feel
as if my mind
is boiling"

We can see that each stanza in the above poem begins with "I don't know", but the second stanza assumes as an already known premise the fact that seemed doubted about in the first one; the third stanza assumes as an already known premise the fact that was doubted about in the second one; and with the third stanza the pattern is cut off, because the power of feelings is so high that a further growth could not be possible (after "my mind is boiling", there could not follow another stanza). There is a feeling of musical crescendo in this poem. In a way, if we think of a book as a special kind of "letter" written by the poet for the reader, this poem might symbolize the relation between the poet and the reader.

The passing of time seems a central element in the whole book. Some poems focus on the time flow, as it may be perceived when contemplating the evolution of society. For example, in the poem "Reading Historical Records", the poet says:

"you can see the river of time keeps rolling forward.
It seems calm and tranquil
but the undercurrents
keep welling up in it."

The above "undercurrents" of history are seen as negative aspects of society and shortcomings of some people, blocking the general progress of mankind. One may find strong irony and satire in such poems. An example is "The Backbone", where direct social criticism is expressed:

"Yet we have never found backbone
among those politicians and literary prostitutes."

The author's strong criticism is directed also against the irresponsible ecological crimes that are happening in our modern world, crimes for which the corrupted or incapable leaders are responsible. Here is a fragment from the poem "Passing by A Placer Deposit":

"The mountain forest has been denuded
Pollution presses on step by step
Ozonosphere has been chiseled
The earth has been drawn empty
Green has been swallowed by concrete
O, Nature! O, human being!
Can you flee?
Where can you flee?"

All these negative aspects of life appear as the so-called "undercurrents" of time, as the poet names them in "Reading Historical Records".

In his Postscript, HSU Chicheng refers to the strong social criticism that appears in his latest works: *"More works of exposing the dark side of things can be found in this book than in any other book I have published before.*

Perhaps this is because I have met with too much dirt since I moved to the city ten more years ago."

Very often, the time flow is presented like in an accelerated movie, in order to create a stronger sense of the caducity of a human being. For example, in the poem "One Who Plays With Fine Sand" the author presents to us a "protagonist", a sort of "movie character" who keeps playing with sand on the beach. And suddenly, the film is accelerated in the last stanza:

> *"Then, wonder appear:*
> *From his hands to his whole body*
> *firstly wrinkles appear*
> *then the old age speckles.*
> *Then he decomposes*
> *and turns into fine sand*
> *in the sandy beach..."*

The above stanza is characteristic for the way Hsu Chicheng sees human rhythmical evolution as part of the rhythm of the whole universe. In many poems there are images of wrinkles, scars and speckles, all of them suggesting the changes in the lives of people, as well as the passing of time. There is only one poem dealing with an unchangeable skin mark, a birthmark that exists as long as a person lives. "Birthmark" is the title of that poem. And Hsu Chicheng thought that image so important, that he named the whole book "Birthmark". In his Postscript, he explains why that poem seemed so important to him. He says: *"I have never sung the praise of the dark side of things, but always spit on and curse them. I will never change the idea that I always persist in, just as what I have written in one of my poems entitled Birthmark"*. After that statement, Hsu Chicheng quotes the last two stanzas of that poem, which I am going to quote too:

> *"Oh, I have come to know*
> *the birthmark was born together with me.*
>
> *Whether it is beautiful or ugly*
> *I am I still*
> *I am always I*
> *I will insist it all my life*

and won't change even a bit
even meeting more hardships…"

It seems to me that the birthmark (which is the central image of the whole book, as it appears in the title) suggests the poet's effort to resist time, to remain he himself in spite of everything.

詩之韻即生命之韻

Luiza Carol 作　　雅靜譯

評許其正的詩集《胎記》2006 年環球文化出版社出版

　　許其正的詩最感動我的是它們特殊的韻律映照出生命的韻律。我沒能對詩節的音律效果予以評論，因為我不懂中文。但英文翻譯幫我對詩人的思想、某些措辭和意象的韻律形貌深具概念。概括地說，我對作者將詩的韻律作為運用於把他自己的特質過度轉化到宇宙的

手法有普遍的感受。詩的韻律可解釋為介於內在韻律
（以文字和文法結構表達心的脈動、呼吸、感情和思想）
和外在世界韻律（自然的季節變化、人一生發展的年齡
改變、社會發展的歷史進程）之間的橋樑。

我們來看一看〈白雲圓舞曲〉這首詩的第一部分。
我們可以在這裡發現六個詩節確切共用相同的文法結
構。我們能追蹤三組重複的意象依如下類型排列：ABC
（第一節），BCD（第二節），CDE（第三節），DEF（第
四節），EFA（第五節），FAB（第六節）。"圓舞曲"的意
象頭尾銜接，暗示季節的變化，每一尾部即為新的開始：

一群白鴿
飛進棉絮裡
月光看見了？
你看見了？

一群棉絮
飛進月光裡
葦花看見了？
你看見了？

一群月光

飛進葦花裡
濃霧看見了？
你看見了？

一群葦花
飛進濃霧裡
細雪看見了？
你看見了？

一群濃霧
飛進細雪裡
白鴿看見了？
你看見了？

一群細雪
飛進白鴿裡
棉絮看見了？
你看見了？

　　在上面的詩節裡，最後重複的問題"你看見了？"，直接邀請讀者受感動參與這形形色色的詩韻變化。隨上舉六節之後的第二部分，讀者會發現相似的意象運用於

不同的韻律，就像相同的舞者舞著一支新的圓舞曲。這
意味著詩中有一支"沒有終結"的舞曲，和其他許多詩一
樣。

　　在〈讀信〉一詩中，寫信者的感情傳導到讀信者身
上，以詩韻律的連結，心情的溫暖由詩傳導了。整首詩
如下：

　　　我不知道是不是
　　　因為情意太過深濃
　　　以致感覺裡，仿佛
　　　每字每句
　　　炙熱燙人

　　　也不知道是不是
　　　因為字句炙熱燙人
　　　以致感覺裡，仿佛
　　　這信這箋
　　　著火狂燃

　　　更不知道是不是
　　　因為信箋著火狂燃
　　　以致感覺裡，仿佛

　　我心我意
　　滾燙沸騰

　　我們可以在上面這首詩中看到每一節用"我不知
道"，但第二節卻假設確已知道第一節裡懷疑的前提這事
實；第三節假設第二節裡懷疑的前提這事實；第三節則
轉移此型態予以切割，因為感情的大力已高漲到不可能
再漲高（在"我心我意/滾燙沸騰"之後已不能再續別的詩
節了）。這首詩中有音樂漸強的感情在。如果我們認為
一本書是詩人寫給讀者的特殊"信件"，這首詩可能象徵
詩人和讀者之間的關係。

　　時間流逝似乎是這本書的中心要點。有些詩聚焦於
時間的流失，仿佛感知對社會發展的沉思。譬如〈翻開
歷史書頁〉，詩人說：

　　便看見時間滾滾而去
　　雖有看似風平浪靜之時
　　卻無時無刻不有起伏
　　只是高低大小不同而已

　　上面所謂歷史的"起伏"一般認為是社會的負面和某
些人的缺失，阻礙了人類的普遍進步。我們可以在這種

詩中看到強烈的譏刺和諷喻。譬如〈脊樑〉就直接指向
對社會的批評：

　　唯獨偎大邊的政客和攀附的文醜
　　在他們身上怎麼搜都搜不到脊樑

　　作者的強烈批判也直指發生在我們現今世界不負
責任的侵害生態犯罪，貪腐和無能的領導者需負責的犯
罪。〈從砂石場邊走過〉詩中就有其斷片：

　　山林被噬於濫墾濫伐之口
　　純淨消瘦於步步進逼的污染
　　臭氧層被鑿開孔洞
　　土地為砂石場所掏空
　　鮮綠被蠶食鯨吞於水泥叢林
　　大自然啊，人類啊
　　你還能逃嗎？
　　你逃到哪裡？

　　所有這些生命的負面就是所謂時間的"起伏"，就是
在〈翻開歷史書頁〉中所指涉的。
　　在後記中，許其正對社會的強烈批判展現在他新的

作品中："這本集子內的作品負面的題材比以前多一些。這可能是因為我遷居到都市裡，十幾年來接觸負面的事物多了。"

時間的流逝，像極流動電影，為了創造人類老邁的強烈感覺。譬如在〈玩沙者〉中，作者帶給我們的"主角"，是一種在海灘玩著沙子的"電影"人物。突然，影帶在最後一節加速進行：

　　　　後來，奇蹟出現了：
　　　　從手開始，以致全身
　　　　他先是起了皺紋
　　　　然後長出老人斑
　　　　終至腐朽崩壞
　　　　散落沙灘上
　　　　碎成細沙……

上舉詩節標舉出許其正將人類詩韻的進展視為全宇宙詩韻的一部分。在許多詩中都有皺紋、傷疤和老人斑的意象，全都暗示人們生命的改變，和時間的消逝一樣。其中有一首描述一個不可改變的皮膚標記，與人的生命同始終的胎記。"胎記"是那首詩的標題。許其正認為那意象甚為重要。他說："我絕不是在頌揚這些負面的事物，而是在唾罵它們。我很有自信，我一向的

理念，我絕不會改變，正如我在'胎記'一詩中所寫
的：

　　原來胎記之於我
　　與生俱來，根深柢固

　　是美也好，是醜也罷
　　我就是我
　　我永遠是我
　　終身堅持到底
　　絕不稍有改變
　　哪怕風雨再大……"

　　我覺得，胎記（正如題目所示，是這本書的中心意
象）似乎暗示詩人努力抗拒時間，不論如何，他要留住
自己。

2010.1.8－15　亞特蘭大新聞「亞城
園地」文學週刊

2010.2.8　世界詩人季刊

2012.11　Breakthrough

按:本文作者為以色列名女詩人，除詩外，兼及兒童文學。

許其正和他的新作

湯爲伯

　　嗜好文藝筆耕的人很多，文才縱橫的人也不少，可是有毅力、有恆心將筆耕的興致，堅持與自己的生活、生命共始終的人卻非常少，我的筆耕的摯友許其正先生，就是極少數將筆耕的興致，堅持與他的生活、生命共始終的典型者。

　　他自 1960 年，二十一歲那年開始踏入文藝園圃的門扉，便深深的迷於文藝，並立誓要長期做文藝園圃裡的耕種者。他發現世間唯有文藝果實是滋養人類心性的最佳補品，也是人類希望的泉源。

　　許先生專心播種兩類文藝種籽，一是新詩，另一是散文。他自踏入文藝園門那日起，文藝園圃範疇內不但是他心神倚託而安怡的家園，並且也等同進德修業的大學府。

　　他在文藝園圃裡沉迷筆耕不覺已逾半世紀時光

了。如此漫長的時光裡，他耕耘的文藝成果與他耕耘的事業成績是雙料豐碩的，無所偏廢。文藝成果方面：他已出版有「半天鳥」等六種詩集，其中有三種又出版中英對照，兩種又出版中希對照，一種又出版漢蒙對照。今（2010）年三月甫由四川環球文化出版社出版的「山不講話」詩集則為中英日三種文字對照，集內納三十五首短詩。

許兄散文亦出版「襪苗」等六種，暢銷國內外。其作品被選入數十種選集，也編有劇本，獲獎多次，2004年被國際詩歌翻譯研究中心選為世界最佳詩人，被列入中華民國現代名人錄、英國劍橋世界名人錄及 21 世紀前 2000 名傑出世界智慧人物名錄，世界藝術文化學院及國際詩歌翻譯研究中心亦各頒發榮譽文學博士學位。

他的學歷與事業方面也是鰲峰獨占：東吳大學法學士、高雄師大研究所結業；曾任編輯與記者、軍法官，任教高職、五專教師及兼任教務主任多年，並在鳳山陸軍官校任文藝創作社團指導教授。

從事培植國家棟樑之才的教職工作，雖然職位不高，但職業極為神聖而偉大。

我與許兄是筆耕文藝的同好，我最羨佩他的還是在文藝方面的輝煌成績。這全靠他恆心與毅力的堅持，因為他是從正業的零碎隙縫中偷暇耕耘的，只能算是消遣娛樂，而他能匯集如此豐碩而優良的文藝成果，實屬不易。

　　許兄以攻詩為重點。他對新詩寫法向來堅持口語化，不故搞九彎十八拐來賣弄技巧，易讀易解，不讓讀者苦思苦想去猜謎。

　　例如今年三月出版的「山不講話」這冊詩集裡的第一首──誰曾打敗過時光：

　　　誰曾打敗過時光？
　　　你嗎？你曾用
　　　石頭、刀、槍甚至最先進的核彈
　　　企圖打敗時光嗎？
　　　但是，結果呢？成功了嗎？

　　　誰曾打敗過時光？
　　　時光手無寸鐵
　　　它卻輕易地打敗你，打敗萬物
　　　令你和萬物一起滿臉皺紋
　　　令你和萬物一起衰頹、腐朽

　　　誰曾打敗過時光？
　　　歷代君王如秦始皇等

他們曾企圖打敗時光，永生不老
但是，最後呢？
他們不是和萬物同朽了嗎？

誰曾打敗過時光？
你是清楚看到了
用什麼力量都沒辦法
用什麼武器都沒辦法
用什麼藥物都沒辦法

誰曾打敗過時光？
告訴你，我看見了
只有他，只有他
用柔軟如水的文字打敗過時光
只有他——詩人

　　當讀者朋友讀完最後一段的結論時，定會恍然瞭悟，原來只有寫詩或讀詩的人才有能力打敗時光。這譬喻當你身心陷於艱苦憂煩的時候，如果能閱讀一首激勵士氣，振奮希望的好詩，或者啟發自己靈感而作出一首鏗鏘有聲的好詩來，保證再如何艱苦憂煩的時光，皆能一掃而光。

例如另一首——秋：

一個懷孕著滿城煙雨的少婦鼓腹蹣跚地走著。
她的金色頭髮蓬鬆地垂在她的雙肩和背上。
她那略帶憂鬱的臉上滿掛著想要落蒂的果子。
很多人看見她。他們問她她所要去的地方。
嗯嗯——她漫不經心地答應著。
她說她要到綠蔭深濃的林子裡去生產。
她說她要去生產一個甜甜胖胖的完美的娃娃。

這首詩的特色，分明是讚頌秋天是農莊農產豐收的景況，但許兄從頭至尾不見一句美景的文字描述，而只是把豐收的秋季形容為一位懷孕即將臨盆的婦人。走進樹林，也許指的是果園，滿園果子皆已成熟了。雖然不見表面華麗的文字描述，但意涵卻極深邃。

另一首題為「山不講話」的詩，我對它特別有興趣：

山不講話
山就是不講話

我從遠處招呼他
他不講話

我走前去親近他
他不講話
我大聲問他
他不講話
……

我賞讀著它，並觸起我的回憶，也激起了我創作散文的靈感。

我童年生長在贛北鄉間，家居後方與左方不到三百公尺處便是山林；由於長時間接觸山林，所以對山的性質甚為熟稔，其實山是會講話的，只是它不主動講話，必須有人引導它講，教導它講它才講話。

當人們走進山的峽谷裡去，開口講話時，山也學習你講話，你講大聲，它也跟著講大聲。你講小聲，它也講小聲。你唱歌，它也唱歌。你罵它，它也回罵你。你笑，它也笑。放牛和拾柴的小兒們最愛引逗山說話和嬉笑了。

上面這一段是題外話，且放過不談。詩的語言與散文，與論文本來就不一樣，不能直接了當。許兄詩的結尾寫著：

我低著頭想

　　想了一下又一下
　　我終於想通了：
　　山最偉大！

　　許兄崇敬山的偉大。山恆久矗立不移，沉默不語，
俯瞰世間千奇百怪，與世態炎涼冷暖，及政爭與紛擾；
但是山依然沉默矗立不移。

　　下面是一首親切、可愛的詩——小孩的臉：

　　小孩的臉是一座花園
　　形形色色的花
　　經常在這裡綻放

　　引來許多眷顧
　　引來許多歡欣
　　引來許多讚美

　　但願這一張臉
　　永遠繁花盛開
　　沒有風雨來干擾破壞

　　中外許多名人格言都形容：人類臉上的笑容，是最

美麗的鮮花。的確，體態儘管多麼優美，滿臉冷酷嚴肅，取不到他人的喜愛，敬鬼神而遠之。

　　讀這首詩時，必須有兩種猜測：一種是想像他真的是一個整天滿臉掛著笑容的幼童，贏得眾多人的喜愛，但願人人也要多多關懷他，愛顧他，莫使他受到意外的傷害與病痛。另一種想像也許是隱喻環境，或者事情，當然只有許作者自己清楚。

　　許兄在多首詩裡提起「蜜子」，且多半是對話或問話，不知是他的舊妻子，或新歡情人？從詩句間看出他倆感情甚篤，可謂如糖似蜜，也如膠似漆，令人羨慕不已。茲例舉其中一首——互握著手：

　　互握著手，蜜子
　　以手指無言地傾吐
　　傾吐全心靈中的愛

　　這是個世界，聲音語言之外的
　　唯心靈在此對語
　　我知道，蜜子，相信你也知道
　　……

　　不用全首抄錄，相信讀者們閱讀以上六句，就能完全瞭解他倆感情有多濃多深了。

　　我與許兄雖然相識有年，但由於我們彼此分住南北兩地，而且職業不同，所以他家中私事我不甚瞭解，因而我也不方便對他的詩作內容妄加揣測。我們只要把彼此辛勤耕種的文藝果實，互贈互賞就心滿意足了。

2010.7.2 亞特蘭大新聞「亞城園地」文學週刊

　　按：湯兄別「虧」我這和你一樣不會找「外食」的老實人。內子名林蜜，不加姓，日文稱為「蜜子」。詩中的「蜜子」就是這樣來的。她人如其名，林蜜台語讀如「飲蜜」，很甜也。每向初見面的人介紹時，我都開這個玩笑，以增加記憶也。想這麼甜蜜的妻子，我珍惜都來不及了，哪來「舊妻子」、「新歡情人」？必也從一而終！

A BOOK REVIEW of "BIRTHMARK"

Dr. Ram   Sharma

"BIRTHMARK":HSU   CHICHENG,   THE
EARTH CULTURE PRESS, U.S.A, 2006, ISBN
0-9637599-6-5/A.012, PRICE : RMB Y=30.00

Poetry is not the product of discussions but it is
overflow of powerful feelings.Hsu Chicheng is a famous
contemporary Chinese poet, writer and translator , native
of Pintung County, Taiwan .He has published five
collections of poems printed in Chinese-English or
Chinese-Greek .He has published six collections of prose
including the one entitled Excellent Seedling. Many of his
poems have been translated into English , Japnese and
Greek.

Chicheng writes about his poems " *Perhaps due to my*

nature , my works is always based on depicting humanity , native land , idyllic life and nature , sings the praise of the bright side of human experience , so as to encourage people to brace themselves up and be bent on doing good." [Postcript]

This poetry collection has 54 poems .Hsu Chicheng appears before us as Chinese William Wordsworth and he presents all his feelings and thoughts .Such poems presents him as worshipper of nature as ' The Sea`s Five Appearances' , ' The Footmarks in the Sandy Beach', ' A Wild Grass`s Account in its own Words' , 'Waterfall'.

There is no need to be surprised
Only there is a bit of earth
I can grow and live on
Even on the roof built with cement
So strong a character I have , that nothing can press me !

（A Wild Grass's Account in its own Words'　p.20~22）

Not only Wordsworth but he presents Shelley`s spirit of delineating the nature .The Poem 'A Waltz of the White

Clouds' remembers us of Shelley`s ' Ode to the West Wind'.

> *A group of cotton wadding*
> *Have flown into the moonlight*
> *Have the reed flowers seen it ?*
> *Have you seen it ?*
>
> (A Waltz of the White Clouds p.66)

The best part of poets Wordsworthian spirit is that he presents not only the description of nature but the philosophy of life. He gives us message of life through his verses.

He advises us to go back in the lap of nature in such poems as 'Morning Dew', 'Going to the Countryside', ' My Afternoon Mood', ' The Mountain Path'.

> *Let`s go to the countryside*
> *And be far away from*
> *The noisy, dirty and bustling city----*
>
> (Going to the Countryside   p.96)

This poetry collection has other types of flowers besides nature like naked realities of life is expressed through these poems 'A Chinese Knot of Emotion', 'The Image of the Time', ' Wrinkles', ' Reading a Letter', ' Powerless Sense', 'An Extempore Verse After Retirement', ' Old Age Speckles'.

Having inhaled the youthful years up
Old age speckles appear one after another
Like dusk
Like the soaks of an old wall

（Old Age Speckles　p. 84）

The poet also forces us to think and to ponder about the present day problems of like through such poems as 'Reading Historical Records', ' Traffic Jams', ' SARS, Saliva', ' Saliva, Quarantine', ' Local Accent', ' Passing by a Placer Deposit'.

I am meeting traffic jams now
Why I often meet traffic jams ?
What will I do ? Unless you don`t live

In a modern metropolis！

（Traffic Jams　p. 108）

These poems were translated from Chinese to English by Yang Zongze skillfully. I think the poet is quite successful in his efforts of communicating his thoughts and this poetry volume is a must read for every avid reader of literature."

評「胎記」

藍姆・薩爾馬作　雅靜譯

《胎記》許其正著，環球文化出版社出版，國際統一書號：ISBN 0-9637599-6-5/A・012

　　詩不是論辯的產物，而是強烈感情的流出品。許其正是一位著名的當代中國詩人、作家和翻譯家，出生於台灣屏東。他已出版了五本中英對照或中希對照的詩集，並已出版了包括書名為「碧苗」的六本散文集。他的許多詩已被譯為英文、日文和希臘文。

　　其正的詩，「許是天生使然，我一直立足人道，寫鄉土、田園、大自然，歌頌人生的光明面，勉人憤發向善。」（後記）

　　這本詩集包括有 54 首詩。許其正以中國的華滋華斯出現在我們面前，展現出他的感情和思想。從「海的五貌」、「腳印・踩在沙灘上」、「野草的自述」和「瀑布」這些詩，可以看出他是一位大自然的愛好者。

> 沒什麼好驚異的
> 只要有一點點土
> 我便能長出來，活存下去
> 即連水泥屋頂不也可看到我？
> 這樣的稟性，誰能壓抑得了？
>
> 　　　　（野草的自述　20~22頁）

　　不僅展現出華滋華斯，他還展現出雪萊對大自然描繪的神韻。「白雲圓舞曲」讓我們記起雪萊的「詠西風」：

> 一群棉絮
> 飛進月光裡
> 葦花看見了？
> 你看見了？
>
> 　　　　（白雲圓舞曲　66頁）

　　詩人許其正的詩最美好的神韻，是他不僅描寫大自然，而且抒發生命的哲學。他透過詩送給我們生命的訊息。

　　他在「朝露」、「走向田園」、「午後心情」和「山路」裡告知我們回到大自然的懷抱。

　　　　走向田園
　　　　遠離城市裡煩人的
　　　　喧囂、緊張、雜亂、汙穢……
　　　　　　　（走向田園　96頁）

　　這本詩集還有其他大自然以外生命真諦的花朵形態表現在「中國結　外解」、「時間的影像」、「皺紋」、「讀信」、「退休即興」和「老人斑」諸詩中。

　　　　吸盡了飛揚的青春
　　　　老人斑以濃濃暮色
　　　　一塊一塊呈現
　　　　形如古牆上的漬痕
　　　　　　　（老人斑　84頁）

　　詩人也透過「翻開歷史書頁」、「塞車」、「SARS·

口水」、「口水‧隔離」、「鄉音」和「從砂石場邊走過」
這些詩，強力驅使我們去深深思考當今的難題。

　　　　又碰到塞車了
　　　　怎麼常常碰到塞車？
　　　　可是又能奈何？誰叫你
　　　　活在現代，活在都市裡？
　　　　　　　　（塞車　108 頁）

　　這些詩由楊宗澤從中文精譯為英文。我認為詩很成
功地盡力傳達出他的思想。這本詩冊是愛好文學的讀者
所必讀的。

　　　　　　　　　　2010.8.8　世界詩人

　　譯者按：藍姆‧薩爾馬（Ram Sarma），1974 年生，印度當
　　　　　　代詩人作家，以英文和亨第文寫作，頗有成就與盛
　　　　　　名。他在當學生時就已有優異表現。他以研究後現
　　　　　　代印度小說獲得博士學位。他是一個著名詩人、文
　　　　　　評家、書評家和翻譯家。他的詩在世界上頗見曝光
　　　　　　率；作品包括研究報告、論文、詩和書評，經常發
　　　　　　表在印度國內外期刊、雜誌和報紙，也經常在印度
　　　　　　諸多網路期刊發表。他現在是印度 J.V.P.G.學院的高
　　　　　　級講師。

許其正的創作歲月

── 兼談其新著《盛開的詩花》

魯 蛟

　　詩人有兩種，一種是埋首於創作；一種是忙著推銷自我。許其正是屬於前者。

許其正是誰

　　一九三九年出生在台灣南端的屏東縣潮州鎮一個不到十戶人家的小農村。青少年時代都是在鄉野田園間過日子；割草、牧牛、玩砂、捏泥、搞耕作、幹農活，樣樣都會。即使後來任職於外地外鄉，一有空還是會回到故鄉來過他溫馨的田園生活。東吳大學法學士、高雄師範大學教研所結業；曾任刊物編輯、記者、軍法官、教師，以及許多文學社團的工作者或是負責人。綜其生平，大概可以用以下的這些句組來說明：

　　他是一個泥土氣味很重的知識人。

　　他是一個二十一歲就在「聯合副刊」上發表詩作的人。

　　他是一個有三十三年歷史的教育工作者。

　　他是一個具有五十餘年歷史的文學創作者。

　　他是一個七十二歲還不服老的剛毅作家。

　　他是一個集創作和翻譯於一身的文學實踐者。

　　他是一個有七本詩集七本散文集的文學人。

　　他是一個文字多於聲音的表達者。

　　他是一個走自己的路耕自己的田的自主者。

　　最重要的是，他強烈的擁抱文學操守和創作良知。

豐富的文學生命

　　台灣的文學作品發表園地之一的「聯合副刊」，是多麼不容易攀登的一處高原。可是，二十一歲的文學青年——莊稼人許其正卻爬上去了。對他來說，除了鼓勵之外，也堅強了他的創作意志；昂揚而豐富的文學生命，便自此展開。那是民國五十年五月二十二日的事情。

　　踏上創作之路的許其正，心意蓬勃，筆力旺

活，三年之後的民國五十三年八月一日，便由葡萄園詩社出版了他的處女詩集《半天鳥》。在那個詩集出版不易也不多的年代，《半天鳥》的問世，曾經引起詩壇的注意，那年，許其正才二十五歲。

接下來，他的創作速度略為緩慢。數年之後，腳步加快，創作高潮再起，而且，詩和散文雙棲。自六十五年至六十八年的三年之間，一口氣出版了四本散文和一本詩。值得注意的是，四本散文有三本是「光啟出版社」出的。當時，「光啟」的招牌亮麗閃爍，聲譽高隆，在它那裡出書是光榮的事情。何況是三本。

二〇〇三年之後，他的文學腳步又踏上了中國大陸，在北京的團結出版社出版了中英對照的詩集《海峽兩岸遊蹤》、在重慶環球文化出版社出版了《胎記》（也是中英對照）。接著，文學觸角又伸向了國際（容後再論）。至今為止，包括重印、翻譯在內，一共出版了十二部詩集和八本散文集。其成績不可謂不豐。

鄉土田園和人道

來自農村的許其正，不管走到哪裡，都有一條無形的感情之線，和他的故鄉與土地相連著，他是一個真正的熱愛鄉土（田園和大自然）、擁抱鄉土、書寫鄉土的文學創作者。他以拙樸但卻敏銳之筆，一點點、一滴滴、一篇篇、一首首的，寫他的故鄉事。我們可以從他的作品裡，看到田野的景色，嗅到泥土的芬芳。特別是散文，是他拿手的表現形式。在他的散文集書名上，就可以看到一切；例如《秧苗》、例如《綠園散記》、例如《綠蔭深處》、《走過牛車路》、以及最近出版的《走過廊仔溝》等都是。

他在描述五六十年前的艱苦和後來的變化時，有什麼事實寫什麼事實；有什麼感受寫什麼感受；苦事不亂寫，好事不偏言。這種堅持，我想是來自於他「人道」的創作理念。任何的一個作者，只要胸懷人道，就不會愧對社會和良知。遺憾的是，我們這個社會上，有些人並非如此！

許其正，許其正，真的是極其正也！

真正的國際詩藝交流者

我常常聽到官方單位、民間社團或是作家個人在談論所謂的國際文學交流的問題，其實是看不到影子摸不到結果的；而詩人許其正，多年來卻以一己之力，在默默的做著這件事情。據我所知和相關資料顯示，除前述在大陸出版的兩本中英對照詩集外，於二〇〇四年十月由希臘雅典克萊諾詩刊出版了中希對照的《海峽兩岸遊蹤》詩集。二〇〇七年五月，由希臘梧桐樹出版社出版了「五文」（希、英、法、義、中）對照的翻譯詩集《心的翅膀》。同年的六月和八月，又由蒙古的阿爾特斯夫特出版和大陸重慶的環球文化出版社，分別出版了《胎記》的中蒙版和中希版。接下來，又於二〇一〇年的三月和七月，分別由重慶環球文化出版社和希臘麗希遜朋出版社出版了中、英、日三語的《山不講話》（詩集）和翻譯詩集《不可預料的》。在我們的詩壇上，我看不到誰能如此。

　　這是一串可觀的「一己之力」的書單。我不知道這些詩集在這些國家和地區到底會發揮多大的交流作用，可是，許其正卻以自己的個人力量，做了。除此之外，他還和許多個國家和地區的詩人，經常保持著聯繫，互通著資訊，也傳遞著台灣的訊息。

詩花永遠盛開

　　今（2012）年的5月，他又以豪邁的氣勢和莊

重的態度，由重慶環球文化出版社出版了大版本的
《盛開的詩花——許其正中英對照詩選》。我之所
以稱之為「大版本」，是因為它是「十六開本窄長
型，封面為三百克銅版卡，內頁為八十克輕型蒙肯
紙，計 382 頁」。這是我看過的最厚重、最典雅、
最有價值的個人詩選集。

　　許其正寫詩五十餘年，成詩上千首，這本詩集
裡的一百五十三首詩，是從他文學生涯前五十年所
有的詩作中精選出來的，其代表性自是當然。尤其
是那些曾經被選當作書名的上上之作如〈半天
鳥〉、〈胎記〉、〈重現〉和〈山不講話〉諸首，
都在其中。因為內容豐富作品量多，恕我無法細
述。至於詩的風格和技巧，讀者自會判斷。

　　既是「中英」，執筆翻譯的人極為重要。該書
的譯者是大陸當代著名文學翻譯家、詩人、學者、
天津師範大學翻譯研究所所長、外國語學院教授張
智中博士。名家手筆，鐵定不凡。

　　許其正曾經多次強調「多寫鄉土、田園、大自
然，歌頌人生的光明面，勉人奮發向上」，而且把
他的這種理念完整的實踐在他的作品中，這是我所
認同的；也和我的創作理念相通相融的，這就是必
須要為他和他的新著說幾句話的理由。

最後我要說的是，七十二歲的許其正，自期「以七十為春」；自許「再次開步走——至少得繼續前進」。這些想法，表達出他晚年的雄心壯志，也宣示了他繼續創作的決心。我在面對他的《盛開的詩花》時，明顯的感受到，在他的文學生命裡，「詩花」將是永遠盛開的。

2012.06 於臺北市※
2012.08.12 更生日報四方文學週刊

按：本文作者本名張騰蛟，名作家，擅寫散文，曾任新聞局主任秘書。

On the Poetry Creation of Hsu Chicheng

（Taiwan）**Lu Jiao**

—Concurrent study on his new poetry collection *Blossoming Blossoms of Poetry*

Poets fall into two categories: those who bury

themselves in writing, and those who are busy promoting the selling of themselves. Mr. Hsu Chicheng, of course, belongs to the former category.

Who is Hsu Chicheng

In 1939 Hsu Chicheng was born in a small village of less than ten households, Chauchou Town, Pingtung County, which is located at the south end of Taiwan. He spent his teen years in the countryside fields: cutting grass, herding, sand playing, mud kneading, as well as tilling and farming. Even when the following years bring him to work in alien lands, Hsu does not forget to return to his native place to relive his pastoral life when there arises the occasion. He gained a bachelor's degree in law from Soochow University, and has been educated at the Teaching & Research Institute of National Kaohsiung Normal University, and he has worked successively as periodical editor, reporter, judge advocate, teacher, as well as worker or person-in-charge of many literary corporations. His life experience may be summed up as follows:

He is a person who is redolent of soil, though not without knowledge;

He is a person who published his maiden work on *United Supplement* at the age of 21;

He is a person who boasts 33 years of teaching;

He is a person who boasts over 50 years of literary creation;

He is a person who refuses to give in to old age at the age of 72;

He is a person who can create and recreate (literary translation);

He is a person who has published 7 collections of poetry and 7 collections of prose pieces;

He is a person who has written more than his speech;

He is a person who always follows his own road;

The most important of all, he is a person who embraces literary integrity and creative conscience.

Rich Literary Life

United Supplement is a literary magazine in Taiwan; it is difficult to get one's work published on it, but the

21-year-old Hsu Chicheng made it. For him, this encouraged him and strengthened his will in literary creation. It is from then on that he began his rich and vigorous literary life. That was on May 22, the fiftieth year of the Republic of China.

Newly stepping on the road of literary creation, Hsu Chicheng is ambitious and vigorous. Three years later, he published his maiden collection of poetry entitled *Half Sky Birds* by Vineyard Poetry Society. At that time, the publication of a poetry collection is not a piece of cake, and *Half Sky Birds* is a stir in the circle of poetry. And Hsu was only 25.

In the years that followed, he slowed down his literary step in creation, until he reached another climax several years later, when he took up prose writing, in addtion to poetry creation. In three years, he published 4 collections of prose and 1 collection of poetry. What deserves our attention is, above all, three of his prose collections were published by KuanhChi Publishing House, a prestigious one at that time, for which Hsu reaped a lot of laurels.

Since 2003, his literary steps began to step on

Mainland China: he published *My Whereabouts on Both Sides of Taiwan Strait*, a Chinese-English version published by the Unity Press in Beijing, and *Birthmark*, another Chinese-English version published by the Earth Culture Press in Chongqing. Furthermore, he goes on international (later in detail). Up to now, he has published 12 collections of poems and 8 collections of prose pieces, including his reprinted versions and translations.

Rurality and Pastoral and Humanity

Hsu Chicheng comes from the countryside, and he is forever connected with it wherever he goes. He is a writer who really loves pastoral scenery and the great nature, who embraces the country soil, and writes about the country soil. Little by little, bit by bit, a piece after another piece, he writes about his hometown with his simple and sharp pen, and we can see country landscape and smell fragrance of soil in his literary composition, particularly prose, in which he is stronger. We can see his pastoral love from the titles of his prose pieces: *Seeds and Ears, Random Thoughts on the Green Garden, In the Depth of Green*

Shade, *Passing by the Oxcart Road,* and his recently published *Passing by the Herdboy's Ditch.*

When describing the hardships of the 50s and 60s of the 20th century and the later changes, he assumes a down-to-earth attitude: he does not exaggerate hardships or good things. His perseverance, I believe, comes from his writing idea of "humanity". A writer with "humanity" does not betray the society and his conscience. But it is a pity that not every writer is such a person.

The literal meaning of Hsu Chicheng is honesty and integrity. Yes, the name is the man.

Communicator of International Art of Poetry in a Real Sense

I often hear official units and non-governmental organizations and individual writers talking about international communication of literature, but all in vain. And Mr. Hsu Chicheng is silently undertaking such a task personally for years. As far as I know, in addtion to the two Chinese-English collections of poetry, Mr. Hsu has also published *My Whereabouts on Both Sides of Taiwan Strait,* a Chinese-Greek collection of poems by Greek Athens Keliano in October, 2004; *The Wings of Heart*, a collection of poems in Greek, English, French, Italian, and Chinese by Greek Pheonix Tree Publishing House in May, 2007; the Chinese-Mongolian version and the Chinese-Greek version of *The Birthmark* respectively by Mongolian Artsoft Publishing House and the Earth Culture Press in Chongqing in June and August of 2007; and respectively in March and July, 2010, his poetry collection entitled *The Mountain Refuses to Talk* in Chinese and English and Japanese was published by the Earth Culture Press in Chongqing and his collection of translated poems entitled *The Unpredictable* was published by Greek Lexitipon Publishing House. In so doing, it seems that Hsu is matchless.

The above list of poetry books have been done by Hsu Chicheng himself and I believe, that they are to exert some influence in the countries or areas where they were published. In addition, he keeps close contact with a lot of poets from various countries and areas, while exchanging poetry information.

Forever Blossoming Are Blossoms of Poetry

In May, 2012, Hsu Chicheng published his *Blossoming Blossoms of Poetry — Selected Poems of Hsu Chicheng (Chinese-English)* by the Earth Culture Press in Chongqing, which is a worldbeater, the most massive, elegant, and valuable collection of poems I have ever seen.

The poetry writing of Hsu Chicheng has been over 50 years, during which more than one thousand poems have been produced. The 153 pieces collected in this book are chosen from his poems through so many years, including some poems which have been used as the titles of poetry collections, such as *Half Sky Birds*, *The Birthmark*, *Reappearance*, and *The Mountain Refuses to Talk*, etc. He has produced many good works with rich content, and I cannot detail it here. As for his style and technique, I believe, readers can make their own judgment.

Since the poetry collection is bilingual, the translator is quite important. And now we see the translator is Zhang Zhizhong, a famous translator, poet, and scholar in contemporary China, and director of the Translation Studies Center of Tianjin Normal University, as well as professor of English at the Foreign Languages College of Tianjin Normal University.

For many times Hsu Chicheng emphasizes that we shall "write more about pastoral life and the great nature, while singing praise of the sunny side of life, so as to encourage people to strive to make progress", and he puts his idea into his writing practice. I associate myself with his idea of writing, and I am glad to put a few words for his new book.

At last, I would like to say that Hsu Chicheng, at 72, takes seventy years as a new spring, and he wants to step further. This shows his ambition and determination in writing in his vale of years. Reading his *Blossoming Blossoms of Poetry — Selected Poems of Hsu Chicheng (Chinese-English)*, I can feel that in his literary life, forever blossoming are blossoms of poetry.

June, 2012 Taipei

Tr. Zhang Zhizhong

2012.11.8 世界詩人(The World Poets Quarterly)
2012.11　　Breakthrough

　　按:本文作者本名張騰蛟,名作家,擅寫詩與散文,曾任新聞局主任秘書。刊於更生日報四方文學週刊的是中文文本,刊於 Breakthrough 的是英文文本,刊於世界詩人的則是中英對照文本。

Time and Evolution

Israel Luiza Carol

(About "Blossoming Blossoms of Poetry" by Hsu Chicheng)

For Hsu Chicheng, poetry is a way of life and a journey towards self realization and growth. One cannot avoid the passing of time, but in order to use the passing of time for achieving a real spiritual growth, one has to struggle consciously and diligently, in various possible ways. Poetry is the main way, that Hsu Chicheng elected for the evolution of his personality. He does not only express his feelings in poetry; by means of poetry, he also contemplates his evolution and teaches himself how to improve his strength, his courage, his generosity. By means of poetry, he sees himself as part of the universe, getting inspiration from everything surrounding him and at the same time radiating inspiration all around him. This collection of poems, selected from all his works, becomes at the same time a balance sheet and a springboard of the poet's life and literary creation, because life and literary creation are seen as one entity.

Many poems express nostalgic feelings about the passing of time. Old experiences come again and again in the poet's mind, and memory makes them more and more colorful, more and more significant, more and more "alive". A beautiful example can be found in the poem "The Call Of The Orchard". Here, the poet recalls a beautiful orchard which he used to visit in his youth, by means of visual aspects *("The rosy door is opened")*, sound aspects *("So that birds' singing could drip from among the leaves/ To gently tap on your ear drum")*, touch aspects *("Sharing layers of coolness of the shade with the cushion of grassland")*, taste and odor aspects *("Gently pluck fruit into your mouth/ Let sweetness and fragrance enshroud you")* and erotic aspects *("Drink your nectar of love with your sweetheart")*. As a whole, the orchard acquires symbolical meaning: the whole poetic work of the author seems a literary orchard whose fruit the reader can enjoy by means of all his or her senses.

Such nostalgic feelings are often associated with a passionate love for the roots of his own life: childhood, as a powerful source of inspiration. In the poem "If I Do Not Grow Up", the poet recalls the days of his childhood, when he was unconscious of the passing of time. He says: *"If I do not grow up, I can/ Laugh heartily, say what I think/ And can speak words from the bottom of my heart/ To enjoy free and innocent pleasure."* In the same poem, the freezing of time is seen in a sort of science-fiction vision of vicious circle: *"If I do not grow up, I can/ Sing 'If I Grow Up' with abandon/ Let there be more space for my growth/ No need to pray in private for 'If I Do Not Grow Up'"*.

Childhood memories are associated with a deep love for his family roots and for the old countryside, which is seen as the root of the modern industrialized society. In the poem "Root-Seeking", the hero is desperately searching for his roots, until... *"Finally he gets the answer/ From within his vein-/ His blood tells him the answer/ The root is DNA"*.

In the symbolical poem "The Prop-Root", the poet sees himself like a prop-root, deeply anchored in the traditions of his land:

"Even if someone laughs at me and treats me as a fool/ Even if someone isolates me and presses me/ I will never mind/ I only persist my on ideal/ I am not a migratory bird/ I love this land/ I will reside here abidingly/ And take root deeply and firmly/ In this land..."

We should remember the verse "I am not a migratory bird" in the above quotation, in order to understand the big range of hues to be find in this collection of poems. On the one hand, Hsu Chicheng feels a need to be anchorite in space and time, nurturing nostalgia for a freezing of time and space in an idyllic childhood. On the other hand, he is able to feel a deep nostalgia for change and movement, for flight, for ascending, for going on stubbornly on his chosen road, in spite of difficulties. This aspiration for flight and expanding space, seems related to his desire for self improvement and conscious growth. The collection is full of birds, butterflies, clouds – all symbols of winged inspiration. In the poem "Spreading The Wings" the joy of a bird escaping its cage is compared with the joy of poetry. I am going to quote the whole poem:

"As soon as the door of the birdcage

Was opened

That bird imprisoned long

Spread its wings

Flew out of the birdcage quickly

Flying towards the distance

Though the wind, the rain and the fiery sun were waiting it ahead...

O! Great!

How happy I feel!

My poetry has been imprisoned long

Now she has also smashed the "birdcage"

Spreading her wings

Singing merrily

Flying towards

A boundless space

Though the wind, the rain and the fiery sun are waiting her ahead...

O! Great!

How happy I feel!"

If flying suggests breaking of one's own limits and conquering of more and more spiritual space, the stubborn walking in twilight and winter suggests the struggle with difficulties of old age. The poet wisely prescribes the beauty of twilight and his vision is full of courage and optimism. His words instigate the reader appreciate the beauty of life during all its seasons and moments of the day. He says: *"One's courage has to be taken in both hands/ To appreciate and draw the colorful sunset glow"* (in the poem "Walking In The Long Lane") and again asserts the same idea: *"To step forward with smiles/ Add colors to the days to come"* (from the poem "The Last Section Of Road").

I thank the poet for his wise and optimistic vision of life, so enthusiastic and so contagious.

時光及其演進

──許其正《盛開的詩花》簡論

露絲·卡羅爾

　　對許其正而言，詩是一種生活方式，一種自我實現和成長之旅。人無法避免時光的流逝，但為了運用流逝的時光去實現真正的精神成長，他必須有意識地以各種可能的方式，而奮力拼搏。詩是許其正藉以演進其個性的主要途徑。他不僅在詩裏表達他的感受，還通過詩來思考時光的演進並教會自己如何提升他的力量，他的勇毅，他的氣度。借助詩，他洞悉了自己是宇宙的一部分，他從圍繞四周的各種事物中攫獲靈感，並從中輻射出靈感。這本詩選，是從他所有作品中精選出來的，同時成為了詩人生命與文學創作的決算表和跳板，因為他把生命和文學創作視為一個實體，

　　　隨著時光的流逝，他的諸多詩作表達了追懷之情。過往的經歷一次又一次撞擊詩人的心靈，記憶催生它們越來越多彩，越來越繁富，越來越"生動"。我們可以在《果樹園的呼喚》一詩裏尋找到美好的例證。在這裏，詩人回憶說，他經由一個美麗的果園去回訪他的青春，從視覺方面（"彩門已經敞開"），從聲音方面（"進來讓鳥語從果樹的枝葉間滴下/然後輕輕敲響你的耳鼓"），從觸覺方面（"和碧茵分啖樹蔭的層層清涼"），從味覺和嗅覺方面（"隨意伸手採取果實放進嘴裏/讓甜蜜和清香搖響你的全身"），並從美感方面（"和你的情人共同醉飲醇美的愛之蜜汁"）。總而言之，果樹園富含象徵意

義：作者所有的詩似乎就是一座結滿果實的可以讓讀者歡享其全部的意味或感覺的文學之園。

這種懷舊情感常常與他對生命根源的熱愛相連：童年，強勁的靈感泉源。在《只要不長大》一詩中，詩人召回了童年的日子，當他尚未知覺到時光的流逝。他說："只要不長大，我便可以/縱聲大笑，有話就說/真誠大膽地坦露肺腑之言/享受無知、'童言無忌'之樂"。在同一首詩裏，凍結的時間被視為一種科幻的旋轉視境："只要不長大，我便可以/盡情地唱'只要我長大'/讓前面成長的空間更大更寬廣/不必在私下祈求'只要不長大'"。

童年的記憶與他對家族根源和故舊鄉間深濃的愛意相連，那是被視為現代工業化社會之根。在《尋根》一詩中，男主角無望地尋找著他的根，直到⋯⋯"最後他在他的脈管裏/找到了答案——/原來血液告訴了他/根就叫 DNA。"

在《大板根》這首象徵詩中，詩人視自己為大板根，深深紮根於祖傳的土地上："即使有人笑我傻，說我笨/甚至孤立我，欺壓我/我都不管/我有我的堅持/我不是那些候鳥/我愛這塊土地/我要住在這裡/要把根釘下去，深深釘下去/釘牢這塊土地⋯⋯"。

為了理解這本詩選中的林林總總，我們理當牢記我

引用的詩句"我不是那些候鳥"。一方面，許其正覺得有
必要在時間和空間裏做一個隱者，滋養被凍結的時間和
空間，追憶田園詩一般美好的童年。另一方面，不管有
多少艱難險阻，他都有能力催動深濃的懷舊之情飛翔、
上升，堅持他選擇的道路。這飛翔和拓展空間的抱負，
似乎與他的自我完善和自覺成長有關。詩選中充滿著
鳥、蝴蝶、雲——全都象徵著有翅膀的靈感。在《展開
翅膀》一詩中，鳥兒逃脫鳥籠的喜悅，與詩的喜悅相應
和。我且引全詩如下：

　　打開鳥籠
　　那隻鬱卒了許久的鳥
　　立即展開翅膀
　　甩開所有的羈絆
　　歡唱著
　　飛向一片無限寬廣的穹蒼
　　儘管前方有風有雨有烈日……

　　哇！多好呀！
　　我大大舒了一口氣

　　我的詩，也鬱卒了許久了

　　一發動，便甩開所有的羈絆
　　展開翅膀
　　歡唱著
　　飛向無限寬廣的空間
　　去盡情遨遊
　　儘管前方有風有雨有烈日……

　　哇！多好呀！
　　我大大舒了一口氣

　　如果飛翔暗示突破一個人的極限，征服更多的精神領域，那麼，堅持走在薄暮和冬天裏，便是表明要與老年的諸多厄運作搏鬥。詩人聰明地描述薄暮的美麗，他的視野則充滿勇氣和樂觀。他的詩句鼓動讀者去欣賞生命之美，在每一個季節，在每一天。他說："還是要勇往直前/去欣賞並彩繪繽紛的晚霞"（《走在長巷裏》），並再次宣示這相同的信念："笑著舉步前行/將日子塗上彩色"（《最後這段路》）。

　　感謝詩人的才智和對生命的樂觀視野，如此熾熱，如此感人。

野鬼 Diablo　譯
2012.11.8　世界詩人
The World Poets Quarterly 2012-11-8

BOOK REVIEW"THE MOUNTAIN DOESN'T SPEAK"

ZACHAROULA GAITANAKI, IWA

"THE MOUNTAIN DOESN'T SPEAK"
Poems by Hsu Chicheng
(Chinese-English-Japanese), pages: 126,
March 2010
Edition by "The Earth Culture Press",
ISBN: 978-0-9637599-6-2/A..090

Dr. HSU CHICHENG was born in 1939. He served as a teacher for 33 years. He has retired. From his childhood he is fond of literature and writing. He has published 6 poetry collections and 6 collections of prose. Many of his poems have been translated into English, Greek and Japanese. He was conferred an honorary doctorate of literature by WAAC/WCP.

"THE MOUNTAIN DOESN'T SPEAK" writes in his

homonymous poem. And continues with the verses:

> *"The mountain doesn't speak*
> *The mountain all doesn't speak*
>
> *I beckon him*
> *He doesn't speak*
> *I go near him*
> *He doesn't speak*
> *I loudly ask him*
> *He doesn't speak*
> *I get angry and give a kick at him*
> *He doesn't speak*
> *With disappointment I go away from him*
> *He still doesn't speak.*
>
> *I think of it in doubt*
> *Over and over*
> *I finally find the answer:*
> *The mountain is greatest,"*　*(page 65)*

One more fantastic piece of poetry is his poem "THE

CHILD'S FACE" (page 64):

> *"The child's face is a garden,*
> *Every kind of flower*
> *Always opens fully here.*
>
> *It attracts many people to look after.*
> *It concentracts   jollification*
> *And glorification.*
>
> *I wish this face were*
> *Always to blossoms*
> *Without any trouble."*

The poet send an optimist message with his poem "LOOKING FORWARD TO SPRING" (page 57) He writes in the final stanza:

> *"Fortunately, it is April now*
> *The snows are thawing*
> *I'm secretly pleased*
> *That next spring is coming."*

On page 50, there is his poem "THE CALL OF THE ORCHARD". He sends a clear, sweet and special invitation:

> *"The rosy door is opened, come in*
> *I am a grown orchard in the South*
> *Calling you in special and sweet words in the South*
> *Come in, please come in*
> *… …..*
>
> *Come in and walk along the path in the orchard*
> *Print your footprint here with love songs*
> *Drink your nectar of love with your sweetheart*
> *Come in, please come in…"*

For Dr. HSU, love is something important too. He emphasizes in his homonymous poem ("LOVE", page 67):

> *"Love is a secret*

and is a kindling
everyone owns it
nobody lacks it."

"THE SMILE" (page 70) gives joy and glitter in eyes. It is like "The spring wind which awakens the earth   /   it looks like the rose which blossoms the beauty   /   it looks like the rainbow which hangs up all the colors / it looks like the well – timed rain which satisfied the thirsty."

The face of his sweetheart is "more beautiful", "AS JUNE COMES" (page 73):

"The steps of summer are approaching
as June comes

The sun shines brighter
the trees and grasses grow greener
the birds sing sweeter
-ha it is better now.

As June comes

my sweetheart, you are more beautiful. "

Dr. HSU CHICHENG treats us optimist poetry, with sentiment and beauty, with light and smile. Though his collection entitled "THE MOUNTAIN DOESN'T SPEAK" his verses speak to our heart and have gained our estimation with their simplicity, the clearness of their senses, the sensibility and their warmth. "THE MOUNTAIN DOESN'T SPEAK" is an important book of poetry.

ΔΙΑΒΑΖΟΝΤΑΣ...

Κριτικά Σημειώματα από τη ΖΑΧΑΡΟΥΛΑ ΓΑΪΤΑΝΑΚΗ

Δρ. Χσου Σισένγκ: «ΤΟ ΒΟΥΝΟ ΔΕΝ ΜΙΛΑΕΙ»
Ποιήματα σε τρεις γλώσσες (Κινέζικα, Αγγλικά & Γιαπωνέζικα)
Σελ.: 126, Μάρτιος 2010, έκδοση του «The Earth Culture Press»

Ο Δρ. ΧΣΟΥ ΣΙΣΕΝΓΚ γεννήθηκε το 1939 στην Ταϊβάν. Εργάστηκε ως δάσκαλος σε σχολεία και κολέγια. Τώρα είναι συνταξιούχος και ζει στην Ταϊπέι. Από την παιδική του ηλικία ασχολείται με τη Λογοτεχνία και το γράψιμο. Εξέδωσε δουλειά του για πρώτη φορά το 1960 και από τότε έχει κυκλοφορήσει αρκετά βιβλία με ποίηση και πεζογραφία. Έχει τιμηθεί διεθνώς για το έργο του. Ποιήματά του έχουν αποδοθεί σε ξένες γλώσσες.

«ΤΟ ΒΟΥΝΟ ΔΕΝ ΜΙΛΑΕΙ» μας λέει ο Δρ. ΧΣΟΥ στο ομώνυμο ποίημά του και συνεχίζει:

«Το βουνό ολόκληρο δεν μιλάει.

Του γνέφω
δεν μιλάει,
πηγαίνω κοντά του
δεν μιλάει,
το ρωτάω μεγαλόφωνα
δεν μιλάει,
θυμώνω και του δίνω μια κλωτσιά

δεν μιλάει,

μ' απογοήτευση φεύγω μακριά του

ακόμα δεν μιλάει.

Τελικά βρίσκω την απάντηση:

το βουνό είναι μέγιστο.» (σελίδα 65)

Ένα ακόμη θαυμάσιο ποίημά του είναι «ΤΟ ΠΡΟΣΩΠΟ ΤΟΥ ΠΑΙΔΙΟΥ», στη σελίδα 64:

«Το παιδικό πρόσωπο είναι ένας κήπος

(όπου) κάθε είδος λουλουδιού

ανοίγει πάντοτε τελείως εκεί.

Προσελκύει πολλούς ανθρώπους

για να το φροντίζουν,

συγκεντρώνει ευθυμία και εξύμνηση.

Εύχομαι αυτό το πρόσωπο να ήταν

πάντα σε άνθιση

χωρίς καμιά ανησυχία.»

Ο ποιητής στέλνει ένα αισιόδοξο μήνυμα με το ποίημά του «ΠΕΡΙΜΕΝΟΝΤΑΣ ΜΕ ΧΑΡΑ ΤΗΝ ΑΝΟΙΞΗ» (σελ. 57), γιατί:

«Ευτυχώς, είναι τώρα Απρίλης,
τα χιόνια λιώνουν,
είμαι κρυφά ευχαριστημένος
που η επόμενη άνοιξη έρχεται.»

Στις σελίδες 50 και 51 υπάρχει το ποίημα «Η ΦΩΝΗ ΤΟΥ ΟΠΩΡΩΝΑ», με μία όμορφη, γλυκιά και ξεχωριστή πρόσκληση:

«Η ροδοκόκκινη πόρτα άνοιξε, έλα μέσα,
είμαι ένας ανεπτυγμένος οπωρώνας στα Νότια,
σε παρακαλώ με ξεχωριστές
και γλυκές λέξεις στα Νότια,
έλα μέσα, παρακαλώ έλα μέσα,
έλα μέσα, παρακαλώ έλα μέσα...
Έλα και περπάτησε κατά μήκος
του μονοπατιού του οπωρώνα,

τύπωσε το αποτύπωμά σου εδώ

με τραγούδια αγάπης,

πιες το νέκταρ της αγάπης

με τον αγαπημένο σου,

έλα μέσα, σε παρακαλώ έλα μέσα...».

Η αγάπη είναι επίσης κάτι σπουδαίο για τον Δρ. ΧΣΟΥ. Λέει στην τελευταία στροφή στο ομώνυμο ποίημά του («ΑΓΑΠΗ», σελ. 67):

«Η αγάπη είναι ένα μυστικό

και είναι ένα άναμμα,

ο καθένας το κατέχει,

κανείς δεν το στερείται.»

«ΤΟ ΧΑΜΟΓΕΛΟ» (σελ. 70), χαρίζει ευτυχία και λάμψη στο πρόσωπο. «Είναι σαν το ανοιξιάτικο αεράκι που ξυπνά (αφυπνίζει) τη γη, μοιάζει με το τριαντάφυλλο, το οποίο ανθίζει την ομορφιά, σαν το ουράνιο τόξο που περιέχει όλα τα χρώματα και σαν την επίκαιρη βροχή που ικανοποίησε τον διψασμένο». Με την ελπίδα πώς το αγαπημένο πρόσωπο θα του χαρίζει συχνά το χαμόγελο, ο ποιητής προσδοκά πώς «η λίμνη της καρδιάς του θ' ακτινοβολεί τα κυματάκια.»

Κι είναι η αγαπημένη μορφή που μοιάζει ωραιότερη «ΚΑΘΩΣ Ο ΙΟΥΝΙΟΣ ΕΡΧΕΤΑΙ» (σελ. 73):

«Τα βήματα του καλοκαιριού που πλησιάζει

καθώς ο Ιούνιος έρχεται.

Ο ήλιος λάμπει φωτεινότερα,
τα δέντρα και τα χορτάρια
αναπτύσσονται πιο πράσινα,
τα πουλιά τραγουδούν γλυκύτερα,
- χα, είναι καλύτερα τώρα.

Καθώς ο Ιούνιος έρχεται, αγαπημένη μου,
είσαι πολύ πιο όμορφη.»

Ποίηση αισιόδοξη, με συναίσθημα και ομορφιά, με φως και χαμόγελο μας κερνά ο Δρ. ΧΣΟΥ ΣΙΣΕΝΓΚ. Αν και η συλλογή του τιτλοφορείται «ΤΟ ΒΟΥΝΟ ΔΕΝ ΜΙΛΑΕΙ», οι στίχοι του μιλάνε στις καρδιές μας και μας κερδίζουν με την απλότητά τους, την καθαρότητα των νοημάτων τους, την ευαισθησία και τη ζεστασιά τους.

«Το Βουνό δεν μιλάει» είναι μια σημαντική ποιητική δουλειά και ο Δρ. ΧΣΟΥ γεννημένος ποιητής κι ένας άνθρωπος με πολλές ευαισθησίες.

ΖΑΧΑΡΟΥΛΑ ΓΑΪΤΑΝΑΚΗ

評許其正的詩集「山不講話」

zacharoula Gaitanaki

雅靜譯

「山不講話」（中英日三語），許其正著，126 頁，2010 年 3 月環球文化出版社出版，國際統一 書號：978－9637599－6－2/A.090

　　許其正，1939 年生。他曾服務教育界 33 年，現在 已退休。從小他就喜愛文學寫作，已出版了 6 本詩集和 6 本散文集。他的許多詩被譯為英文、希臘文、蒙古文

和日文。他曾榮獲世界藝術文化學院及世界詩人大會榮
譽文學博士學位。

　「山不講話」出自他的同名詩。他寫著：

　　山不講話
　　山就是不講話

　　我從遠處招呼他
　　他不講話
　　我走前去親近他
　　他不講話
　　我大聲問他
　　他不講話
　　我氣得踹他一腳
　　他還是不講話
　　我只得失望地離開他
　　他還是不講話

　　我偏著頭想
　　想了一下又一下
　　我終於想通了：
　　山最偉大

（第65頁）

他的「小孩的臉」（第64頁）一詩更具奇想：

　　小孩的臉是一座花園
　　形形色色的花
　　經常在這裡綻放

　　引來許多眷顧
　　引來許多歡欣
　　引來許多讚美

　　但願這一張臉
　　永遠繁花盛放
　　沒有風雨來干擾破壞

　　詩人在他的「春望」（第57頁）一詩中，透顯出樂觀的訊息。他在最後一節寫道：

　　所幸
　　現在已是四月
　　看見部分雪融

我心竊喜
還有第二春

在第 50 頁，有他的詩「果樹園的呼喚」。他在那裡
透顯出亮麗、甜蜜而特殊的邀請：

彩門已經敞開，進來吧
我是一南方成熟了的果樹園
用南方特有的溫馨的語言呼喚你
進來吧，請你進來這裡
……

進來漫步在果樹間的小徑上
和你的情人齊把情歌的腳印印下
和你的情人共同醉飲醇美的愛之蜜汁
進來吧，請你進來這裡

對許博士來說，愛情也是很重要的。他在它名為「愛
情」（第 67 頁）一詩中，特別強調：

愛情是一件秘密
愛情是一星火種

　　誰都珍藏著有它
　　誰都不會缺乏它

　　「微笑」透顯出眼中的喜悅和火花。它像「是春風，
吹醒了大地 / 是玫瑰，綻放了美 / 是彩虹，懸以七彩
繽紛 / 是及時雨，滿足了渴欲」。

　　他的情人的臉是「很美的」，正如「進入六月」（第
73 頁）所寫：

　　進入六月
　　夏天的足音更近了

　　進口六月
　　陽光更明亮了
　　草木更翠綠了
　　──哈，漸入佳境了

　　進入六月
　　蜜子，妳更美了

　　許其正博士用感性和美，光和微笑，饗我們以樂觀
的詩。他的詩集「山不講話」中的詩，詩句深中我們的

心坎，以簡樸，明朗的意識，感性和溫馨，激起我們的
尊崇。「山不講話」是一本重要的詩集。

2011.11.8　世界詩人
2012.11　　Breakthrough

Book review of Blossoming Blossoms of Poetry

Dr. R.K. Singh

Hsu Chicheng. Blossoming Blossoms of Poetry: Selected Poems of Hsu Chicheng (Chinese – English). Translated by Prof. Zhang Zhizhong. Chongqing City : The Earth Culture Press (USA), 2012. Pages 382. Price CNY 50.00, US $ 25.00. ISBN 978-0-963 7599-6-2 /E.009

The volume of Selected Poems of Hsu Chicheng seeks to present his poetic excellence, or, as the poet would like to say, "a new starting point" in his life after 70. Hsu Chicheng has been writing poetry for the past five decades, celebrating nature and humanity: His poems depict native landscape, idyllic life, and human values with respect for Chinese tradition and culture:

"—I am determined to devote myself to human beings

And I don't care about whether you eat up my flesh or drink up my blood." (p. 361)

And

"The fire of strength shall never die out

And shall burn more wildly, wildly..." (p. 359)

Since I do not know Chinese, I cannot say whether he follows the traditional Chinese poetic forms and styles, too, but he is modern in his outlook and true to his personal experiences and vision. As he notes in his prefatory:

"My pieces are written in more blood than in ink. Humanism is the basic point in my writing, with the usual subjects of countryside, landscape, and nature, to eulogize the sunny side of human life and to spur people onward, so as to finally bring benefit to my readers... In the past 50 years, the poetry forum of Taiwan has been an animated scene: various styles and various schools of poems. But I do not follow any other school than my own pastoral school. I go my own way by tilling my own land, sowing my own seeds, and cultivating my own crops...." (p 13)

Obviously, Hsu Chicheng writes with a commitment. His poetic sensibility is rooted in nature, the sea and rivers, the hills and mountains, the winds and rains, the fields and agricultural activities, the docile domestic birds and animals, the sincerity and simplicity of the rural folks, their honesty and tolerance, and the hardships of rural and urban life, etc. He is also aware of the transitions experienced at various points of time in his career as teacher, journalist, military judge, and post-retirement pursuits as a poet, translator and editor. His poetic imagination exudes a sense of history.

While he puts up with challenges of various sociopolitical nature and ups and downs in his own life, his visionary orientation is 'self'-ward despite the disappointing political and economic climate outside. The fighter in him exhorts: *"Hold fast to the will/Never let go of the target/Afraid of no bitterness/Afraid of no loneliness/He shall go his own way by himself alone/To tread ruggedness even/To dispel haze/Walking out of winds and rains/To embrace sunshine"* p. 357), just as the meditator in him rejoices: *"Sitting silent/Quietude is here/Quietude accompanies me/Only two: she and me"* (p 369). Hsu yearns for peace and enjoys it through inner quietude "in the depth of night".

In fact poetry is his spiritual aspiration and fulfillment.

At 73, Hsu exults in hope and faith:

> *"There is nothing bad about retirement*
> *There is nothing bad about dusk*
> *I can paint still*
> *—Though it is painting the afterglow*
> *It can paint better"* (p. 165)

and

> *"Now dusk! Twilight is gathering*
> *What is the length of the long lane ahead?*
> *Is the lane smooth or hard of walking?*
> *In spite of uncertainty*
> *In spite of tiredness and difficulty in walking*
> *No stop and no rest*

One's courage has to be taken in both hands
To appreciate and draw the colorful sunset glow" (p. 475)

and

"Still he does not abandon his hope
He is on the seeking without sparing any effort (p. 367)

Hsu loves brightness (p 355) and sees hope in winter,"Never lose your faith/And wait patiently" (p. 353),as he says. To him, aging is a bliss, a new opportunity:

"This time to be more steady and more steadfast
Spiritually oneself must be thoroughly remoulded
To overcome corporeal aging
To shoulder the load of years
To be walking in scorching heat, severe coldness, and winds & rains

To overstep myriads of hills and rills, as well as bumpiness of roads...."

('Seventy Years as Spring', p. 351)

and

"We raise our heads and overlook, expecting another world

We raise our heads and overlook, expecting another spring"

('Reappearance', p. 347)

Hsu Chicheng as a sensitive observer of himself, others, and nature, voices a free spirit with awareness of the cycle of changes and memories of childhood, growth, and aging. His poems are as genuine as his silvery hair and keep the fire of hope and faith burning (cf. pp. 333, 299, 271, 257).

Poet editor Prof. Zhang Zhizhong's word for word literal translation, as it seems to me, successfully shows the growth of Hsu's mind and personality and places him in the forefront of contemporary Chinese poetry. He is ably joined by a couple of other translator poets, namely Yang Zongze, Yang Xu, and Hsu Chicheng himself who translate some of the best poems in the collection. I also feel that with their close reading of Hsu's poetic texts and/or their presentation in true contexts, Prof. Zhang Zhizhong and others have helped open up new spaces in Chinese poetry, be it from main land China , or from Hong Kong and Taiwan . The translators deserve congrats for their expert rendering of Hsu's inspiring and refreshing texts and contexts.

書　評

R. K. 辛格

　　《盛開的詩花：許其正中英對照詩選》，許其正著，　張智中　教授英譯，重慶：環球文化出版社（美國），　2012 年出版，382 頁，定價：人民幣 50.00，美元 25.00. 書號：ISBN 978-0-963 7599-6-2 /E.009

　　《盛開的詩花：許其正中英對照詩選》試圖展現詩人的詩歌才能，或者正如詩人所言：為了他 70 歲之後人生的"新起點"。許其正寫詩長達 50 年之久，歌唱自然

和人性；他的詩描寫了家鄉的景色、田園的生活、人生
的價值，以及中國的傳統和文化。

> "任你撕去身心吸去血，
> 我只是一心想貢獻給人類！"（361頁）
> 以及：
> "力量之火便永遠不會熄滅
> 而且可能越燒越旺，越燒越旺……"（359頁）

　　我不懂漢語，所以不知道詩人是否遵循了傳統漢語
詩歌的形式和風格，但他的觀點是現代的，並且忠於自
己的個人經歷和視野。他在前言中寫到：

> "我所寫的，……說是以血寫成的，實不為過。
> 我寫作一直以人道為基點，多寫鄉土、田園、大自
> 然，歌頌人生的光明面，勉人奮發向上，有益於世
> 道人生。……這50年來，臺灣詩壇紛紛擾擾，有這
> 個派那個派，許多人合縱連橫，各據山頭，我則不
> 予理會，一直堅守'田園'，'走自己的路'，耕自己的
> 地，播自己的種，培植自己的作物。"　（13頁）

　　顯然，許其正的寫作帶著一種使命感。其詩歌的敏感，植根於大自然：大江大海，山峰高嵐，風風雨雨，田野農活，家禽牲畜，鄉村民間的真誠、淳樸、容忍，以及城鄉生活的艱難，等等。在人生的不同階段，他意識到了自己角色的轉換：教師，記者，軍事法官，以及退休後的追求：詩人、翻譯和編輯。在他詩歌的想像力中，有著一種歷史感。

　　面對來自各種社會政治本質的挑戰以及自身生活中的大起大落之外，詩人的視力定位是朝向"自我"的，雖然外面的政治和經濟氣候令人頗感失望。戰士的本性告誡他："握緊意志／對準目標／再苦都不怕／再孤獨也無所謂／自己一個人走自己的路／把崎嶇踩平／把陰霾驅散／走出風雨／去把陽光擁抱"（357 頁）。沉思者的本性令他欣喜："靜坐／寧靜就在這裏／寧靜就在我左右／只有她和我，我們兩個"（369頁）。許其正渴望和平，"在這寧靜的夜裏"，他用內心的寧靜來享受和平。

　　其實，詩歌是他的精神追求和價值實現。

　　在 73 歲高齡，他仍滿懷希望和信念：

　　　"退休沒什麼不好

　　　黃昏沒什麼不好

　　　我照樣可以彩繪

——雖則彩繪的是晚霞

卻能彩繪得更為美好"（165頁）

和：

"黃昏了！暮色逐步籠罩

前方還有多長的路要走？

前方的路是好走還是難走？

雖然不能確定

但是，不管有多累多難走

還是不得停下來休息

還是要勇往直前

去欣賞並彩繪五彩繽紛的晚霞"（475頁）

和：

"他仍不放棄希望

更用盡心力不停地尋找

……"（367頁）

許其正熱愛光明（355頁），在冬天便看到了希望，他說："別失去信心/要耐心地等待"（353頁）。對他來說，衰老是一種祝福，是一種新的機遇：

"這次會更堅實更穩健
這次不僅是重現，更是重生
精神上必須脫胎換骨
以克服肉體的老化
肩起歲月的重量
穿行在酷熱、嚴寒和風雨中
跨越過所有千山萬水，崎嶇不平……"

（《以七十為春》，351頁）

和：

"我們引頸而望，但願望出一個天地來
我們引頸而望，但願望出一個春天來"

（《重現》，347頁）

許其正是一位敏銳的觀察者，他觀察著他自己、他人、大自然，他表達了一種自由的精神，這種精神意識到了迴圈變化、孩童的記憶、成長和衰老。他的詩，就像他的銀髮一樣真誠，並點燃希望和信念之火（參見 333, 299, 271, 257 頁）。

詩人 張智中教授的翻譯，在我看來，幾乎是一種字對字的直譯，成功地展示了許其正思想和個性的成長，並將其放置於中國當代詩壇的前列。與譯者張智中巧妙配合的，還有幾位詩人譯者，即楊宗澤、楊虛和許其正，許本人翻譯了詩集中的一些上乘之作。同時，我還感到，通過對許其正詩歌文本的細讀和/或在真實上下文中的再現，張智中教授和其他譯者在中國詩歌中開創了一些新的空間：或者來自中國大陸，或者來自香港和臺灣。詩集的譯者們值得祝賀，因為他們成功地再現了許其正詩歌中靈感激發、耳目一新的文本和語境。

（張智中　譯）

The World Poets Quarterly 2013.02.08
2013.02.08 世界詩人季刊

AN ODE TO POETRY

Dr. HSU CHICHENG's new book entitled "Blossoming Blossoms of Poetry" (translated by Zhang Zhizhong), contents his selected poems (Chinese - English) which he has written 50 years. His poems, as the Greek poet Dr. Potis Katrakis writes: "spread perfumes and make life joyful", touches our hearts and our souls.

Poetry is everywhere in his collection. He sings the life, love, nature, women and men, the human relationships, the peace, joys and pains, thoughts, visions, memories, hopes... The poet is a philosopher of life. Sometimes he is pessimistic and sometimes he is optimistic. His style is realistic, personal, honest. Every poem has its own message...

Dr. HSU CHICHENG isn't simply a good poet, frankly speaking, he is a great poet. With his poetry contributes a precious small stone to the structure of

Chinese and international Literature. I thank him with all my heart for this book and I wish him every personal and literary success.

ZACHAROULA   GAITANAKI
Δρ. Χσου Σισένγκ: «Ανθισμένα άνθη της Ποίησης»

ΜΙΑ ΩΔΗ ΣΤΗΝ ΠΟΙΗΣΗ

Το νέο βιβλίο του Δρ. ΧΣΟΥ ΣΙΣΕΝΓΚ με τον τίτλο «ΑΝΘΙΣΜΕΝΑ ΑΝΘΗ ΤΗΣ ΠΟΙΗΣΗΣ» (σε αγγλική μετάφραση του Ζανγκ Ζιζόνγκ), περιέχει επίλεκτα ποιήματά του, τα οποία έγραψε μέσα σε πενήντα χρόνια. Τα ποιήματά του, όπως γράφει και ο Έλληνας ποιητής Δρ. Πότης Κατράκης «σκορπούν ευωδιές και κάνουν τη ζωή χαρούμενη», αγγίζουν τις καρδιές και τις ψυχές μας.

Η ποίηση είναι παντού παρούσα στην συλλογή του. Τραγουδά τη ζωή, την αγάπη, τη φύση, γυναίκες και άντρες, τις ανθρώπινες σχέσεις, την ειρήνη, χαρές και πόνους, σκέψεις, οράματα, αναμνήσεις, ελπίδες... Ο ποιητής είναι ένας φιλόσοφος της ζωής. Κάποιες φορές είναι απαισιόδοξος και άλλες φορές είναι αισιόδοξος. Το στυλ του είναι ρεαλιστικό, προσωπικό, ειλικρινές. Κάθε ποίημα έχει το δικό του μήνυμα...

Ο Δρ. ΧΣΟΥ ΣΙΣΕΝΓΚ δεν είναι απλώς ένας καλός ποιητής, είναι ένας μεγάλος, ένας σπουδαίος ποιητής. Με την ποίησή του βάζει ένα πολύτιμο πετραδάκι στο οικοδόμημα της κινέζικης αλλά και της διεθνούς Λογοτεχνίας. Τον ευχαριστώ για την προσφορά του βιβλίου του και του εύχομαι κάθε προσωπική και λογοτεχνική επιτυχία.

ΖΑΧΑΡΟΥΛΑ ΓΑΪΤΑΝΑΚΗ

2013 年 2 月 8 日世界詩人

詩的讚頌

札塔露拉・格坦娜契

雅靜譯

　　許其正博士的詩集《盛開的詩花》，含括他寫了五十年的詩。他的詩，正如希臘詩人波替斯・卡特拉契斯說的「噴灑出香味，讓生命歡樂」，深深感動我們的心靈和精神。

　　集中到處充滿詩意。他歌唱生命、愛自然、婦女和男士、人際關係、和平、歡樂和痛苦、思想、夢幻、記憶、希望……。詩人是生命的哲學家。他時而悲觀，時而樂觀。他的風格是寫實的、個人的、誠懇的。每首詩都透出訊息……。

　　許其正博士不僅是個詩人，直白地說，是個偉大的詩人。他的詩奉獻給中國詩壇和世界文學以一塊珍貴的小石頭。我全心感謝他的書，並祝福他在個人和文學的成功。

詩人許其正專訪

馬爾他網路 IL-PONT 詩誌

　　編者按：該詩誌為馬爾他著名詩人Patrick J. Sammut所創辦，以馬爾他文及英文印行，發行頗廣泛，遍及全世界。此次該刊於9月初出版，以兩頁刊出對詩人許其正的專訪，簡介部分為馬爾他文，專訪部分為英文，另一頁以英文刊登許其正的定位一詩及照片兩張。本刊特加中譯刊出。定位一詩則附許氏中文原詩。

AN INTERVIEW WITH POET
HSU CHICHENG:

Hsu Chicheng, li twieled fl-1939, huwa poeta Ċiniż kontemporanju. Huwa jikteb u jittraduċi, nattiv tal-kontea Pingtung fit-Taiwan; kiseb Baċellerat fil-Liġi mill-Università Soochow; aktar tard kompla l-istudji tiegħu fl-Istitut tal-Edukazzjoni tal-*Kaohsiung Normal University*. Kien editur, ġurnalist, ġudikatur militari, għalliem u direttur *part-time*, u membru ewlieni u għalliem gwida ta' għadd ta' organizzazzjonijiet tal-arti u l-letteratura. Għallem għal 33 sena u llum huwa rtirat. Sa minn żmien tfulitu kellu għal qalbu l-letteratura u l-kitba. Beda jippubblika xogħlijietu sa mill-1960, bosta minnhom poeżiji u proża, fejn ipinġi art twelidu, ħajja u natura idillika, u jkanta u jfaħħar in-naħa s-sabiħa tal-esperjenza umana. Dan jagħmlu biex iħeġġeġ lill-bnedmin biex jingħaqdu flimkien u jagħmlu ħwejjeġ tajbin. Ippubblika ħdax-il ġabra ta' poeżiji, inkluż *Half Sky Birds*, u oħrajn ippubblikati fl-ilsna Ċiniż-Ingliż, Ċiniż-Grieg, Ċiniż-Mongolu, u Ċiniż-Ingliż-Ġappuniż. Ippubblika wkoll disa' ġabriet ta' proża, inkluż *Excellent Seedling*, flimkien ma' żewġ traduzzjonijiet. Ħafna mill-poeżiji tiegħu ġew tradotti f'bosta ilsna u inklużi f'għadd ta' antoloġiji poetiċi. Ix-xogħlijiet ta' proża u teatrali rebbħuh għadd ta' premji, u ismu huwa inkluż f'pubblikazzjonijiet bħal-lista ta'

Celebrities of The Republic of China, Who's Who? u *2000 Outstanding Intellectuals of the 21st Century*, it-tnejn ippubblikati miċ-Ċentru Internazzjonali tal-Bijografija f'Cambridge, l-Ingilterra. Kiseb dottorati onorarji fil-qasam tal-letteratura, fosthom mill-*U.S. World Academy of Arts and Culture,* u ngħata l-premju kommemorattiv mill-Klabb Letterarju "Xasteron", fil-Greċja, u l-premju onorarju *Naji Naaman* fil-Lebanon. Ġie nnominat għall-Premju Nobel fil-Letteratura, 2014. Hsu ChiCheng illum hu konsulent *part-time* tal-"Large Ocean Quarterly", editor taċ-"Chinese Modern Poetry Quarterly", l-editur ewlieni ta' "The World Poets Quarterly", u president tal-fergħa f'Taiwan tal-*Cai Hong Ying Pen Society*, fl-Awstralja. Huwa membru tal-*International Writers and Artists Association*, u membru onorarju tal-Klabb Letterarju "Xasteron", fil-Greċja.

Describe in brief your native country Pingtung County, Taiwan.

My native country Pingtung County is in the south of Taiwan. The residents are almost peasants, especially of the village I born and grew up. It doesn't above 10 families. We plant paddy, beans, vegetables, bamboo, sugar cane and fruits etc. It's a paradise out of the mortal world in my mind.

Can you share with us some of the memories or episodes you recall from your childhood days?

I'm happy and free in my childhood days. I often bare myself to play and run all over my village and field around it. I then went to graze the cattle and worked in the field as well as played games with child friends.There full of sunshine. I enjoy the pleasure of life with the fragrance of the soil and sunshine, trees and grasses as well as the insects, birds etc..

How was your 33-year old teaching career? Did this contribute in making you a better human being and a better poet?

I went to be a teacher after finished my university education. Teaching career is a great business. A teacher can contact with many younger and guide them to be the grace person and have some more achievements. That interested and brought me joyful. At the same time, I learned from them many things, just as the vividness that made me feel young.

Which were your childhood favourite readings? Which authors/books/poets did you read and love later on in your life?

I almost haven't read many books during my childhood. However, I liked to read many books after 17 of age. There are many books I love to read, for instant, Analects of Confucius, Mencius, Laozi, Zhuangzi etc. of the ancient works of China, prose verse collections as *Stray Birds*, *Fireflies* by Rabindranath Tagore, *The Platero Y Yo* by Juan

Ramon Jimenez, and the works of Johann Wolfgang Von Goethe etc..

You give great importance to nature and the good in human beings in your poems? Why is this? How is this more important today than in older days?

Since I born and grown in the countryside, I love nature inborn. So I give great importance to nature and good in human beings in my poems as well as my prose. I believe all things in the universe are equal and will coexist. Otherwise, I hope human beings must live with peace. I pray all human beings be good in their mind. This point of view is more important today than in old days.

Which style do you prefer: traditional verse or free verse?

I prefer to free verse.

What do you say about the appeal to the different senses, colour and sound in poetry?

No matter what senses, colour and sound in poetry, if a poem touches me.

許其正簡介

許其正,中國當代傑出的詩人、作家、翻譯家。臺灣屏東縣人,1939 年生,東吳大學法學士,高雄師範大學教研所結業;曾任編輯、記者、軍法官、教師兼部分文學社團負責人、指導教師等，以擔任教師時間最久，從五專、高職到國中，共計 33 年，其間並兼任教務主任 13 年；現在已退休。

許氏自小對文藝及寫作具有興趣，於 1960 年開始發表作品，以新詩與散文為主，多寫鄉土、田園、大自然，歌頌人生光明面，勉人奮發向上；已出版《半天鳥》等 12 本新詩集（其中 4 本為中英對照，2 本為中希對照，1 本為中蒙對照、1 本為中英日對照）、《穟苗》等 8 本散文集及 2 本翻譯；作品被譯成英文、日文、希臘文、蒙古文、希伯來文、俄文、法文、葡萄牙文與馬爾他文，被選入近百種選集，詩、散文及劇本曾多次得獎，列名《中華民國現代名人錄》、英國康橋世界名人傳記中心出版《世界名人錄》及《21 世紀世界 2000 名傑出智慧人物名錄》，獲國際詩歌翻譯研究中心頒發榮譽文學博士學位及 2004 年最佳國際詩人，美國世界文化藝術學院頒發榮譽文學博士，國際作家藝術家協會頒發榮譽人文博士及英譯中最佳翻譯，希臘札斯特朗文學會頒發紀念獎，黎巴嫩耐吉‧阿曼文學獎頒發詩歌榮譽獎，另被提名為 2014 年度諾貝爾文學獎候選人。

他現在專事閱讀與寫作，作品以中、英、日、希臘、蒙古等語文，在國內外報紙、雜誌發表，並兼任《大海洋詩雜誌》顧問、《華文現代詩》編委及《世界詩人》混語詩刊（原則上為中英雙語，必要時增加其他國家如法、意、俄、希臘、拉丁等語）特約總編，澳洲彩虹鸚筆會臺灣分會會長，國際作家藝術家協會會員，希臘札斯特朗文學會榮譽會員。

專訪文本

請簡單敘述一下你的故鄉台灣屏東縣。

我的故鄉屏東縣是在南台灣。居民幾乎是農人，尤其我出生長大的村子。它沒超過十戶人家。我們種稻米、豆子、蔬菜、竹子、甘蔗和水果等。在我心中，它是世界上的一個天堂。

你能讓我們分享你童年回憶裡的一些記憶和插曲嗎？

我童年時很快樂而自由自在。我經常打赤膊跑遍玩遍我的整個村子和附近田野。然後當我稍長，我就去放牛，到田裡工作，並和童伴玩各種遊戲。那裡滿是陽光。我欣喜地享受泥土和陽光的芳香，草木以及諸多昆蟲等等……。

三十三年的教學生活如何？這對你成為一個更完善的人和詩人有助益嗎？

我於完成大學學業就去當了老師。教學生涯是一件大事業。一名教師能接觸許多年輕人，引導他們成為有用的人，有所成就。那對我很有趣，帶給我喜悅。同時，我向他們學到好些事，譬如學到活力，使自己年輕。

你小時最喜愛的讀物是什麼？其後你閱讀並喜愛哪些作者、書本和詩人？

童年時我幾乎沒讀什麼書。但是，十七歲後我讀了很多書。有許多書我喜愛去讀，例如中國的古典孔子的論語、孟子、老子、莊子等，泰戈爾的散文詩「飄鳥集」、「螢」、希梅泥茲的「布拉特羅與我」以及歌德的作品等。

你的詩裡很注重大自然和人類的良善？為什麼？在現代，這比舊時代重要嗎？

因為我在鄉間農村出生長大，我天生喜愛大自然。所以我在詩和散文中給予大自然和人性的良善很大的地位。我相信宇宙萬物生而平等且相互共存。另一方面，我希望人類和平相處。我祈望人類內心都良善。這個觀點現代比古代更重要。

古典詩和自由詩，你比較喜歡哪個？

我比較喜愛自由詩。

詩裡的感情、色彩和聲音，哪一個比較吸引你？

不管詩裡的感情、色彩和聲音，只要能感動我都喜愛。

詩一首

ORIENTATION

After their death, no emperors and ministers are immortal

Those who are earnest and do not seek fame, get their fame

Why is the reason behind?
Is it the Creator is joking on us?

Who can set the orientation of a person?
He who is wealthy and powerful?
The powerful with their power
The wealthy with their wealth
Thus can they set their orientation?

Or who can set the orientation of a person?
Geomancers?
Under special invitation
They choose a valuable land with a good geomantic omen
But can they set the orientation of a dead person?

Who can set the orientation of a person?
HSU CHICHENG
Iċ-Ċina

定位 許其正

帝王將相沒幾個死後能夠不朽
真正付出者不刻意營求卻能留芳

這是為什麼？
難道是造物在故意開玩笑？

誰能為一個人定位？
有權勢有財富的人嗎？
有權勢的人以其權勢
有財富的人以其財富
他們這就能為自己定位了嗎？

不然誰能為一個人定位呢？
風水師傅嗎？
他們專門接受委請
以羅盤選取風水寶穴
這就能為死者定位了嗎？

誰能為一個人定位？

2018/11/20 華文現代詩